Physical Characteristics of the Italian Greyhound

(from the American Kennel Club breed standard)

Body: Of medium length, short coupled; high at withers, back curved and drooping at hindquarters, the highest point of curve at start of loin, creating a definite tuck-up at flanks.

Tail: Slender and tapering to a curved end, long enough to reach the hock; set low, carried low.

Hindquarters: Long, well-muscled thigh; hind legs parallel when viewed from behind, hocks well let down, well-bent stifle.

Color: Any color and markings are acceptable except brindle markings and the tan markings normally found on black-and-tan dogs.

Size: Height at withers, ideally 13 inches to 15 inches.

Feet: Harefoot with well-arched toes.

Italian Greyhound

◆

By Dino Mazzanti

CONTENTS

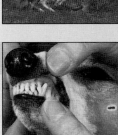

KENNEL CLUB BOOKS® **ITALIAN GREYHOUND**
ISBN 13: 978-1-59378-316-7

Copyright © 2003, 2009 • Kennel Club Books® a Division of BowTie, Inc.
40 Broad Street, Freehold, New Jersey 07728 USA
Cover Design Patented: US 6,435,559 B2 • Printed in South Korea

PHOTOGRAPHS BY MARY BLOOM AND ISABELLE FRANÇAIS
with additional photos by Norvia Behling, T. J. Calhoun, Carolina Biological Supply, Richard Branchaud, Doskocil, James Hayden-Yoav, James R. Hayden, RBP, A. Jemolo, Carol Ann Johnson, Bill Jonas, Dwight R. Kuhn, Dr. Dennis Kunkel, Mikki Pet Products, Phototake, Jean Claude Revy, Alice Roche, Shot on Site Photography, Dr. Andrew Spielman and Alice van Kempen.

ILLUSTRATIONS BY RENÉE LOW.

The publisher wishes to thank Cecilia Amen, Patricia Campbell, Sandy Cornell, Kerri Gelish, Mary Hudson, Sondra Katz, Richard & Pat Klinger, Joan Proto, Gundrun Rosenbush, Laura Thompson and the rest of the owners of the dogs featured in this book.

For a diminutive dog, the Italian Greyhound is an athletic, lithe sighthound who is equally comfortable posing on a pillow as he is chasing a rabbit or participating in coursing events.

HISTORY OF THE
ITALIAN GREYHOUND

The Italian Greyhound is one of the oldest miniature sighthounds in existence, believed to have originated more than 2,000 years ago. The Italian Greyhound's appealing lines and unmatched loyalty have helped sustain its popularity for thousands of years. The breed was favored for many generations by the nobility on various continents. In fact, remains of miniature Greyhound-like sighthounds have even been recovered in Egyptian tombs. These Greyhound-like skeletal structures found throughout the Mediterranean basin help support the nearly world-wide theory of the breed's origin.

Despite popular belief, the breed did not originate in Italy, but may have actually developed in the countries known today as Greece and Turkey. The breed derives its name from Italy partly because it was frequently portrayed in paintings and statues by famous Italian artists. It took until the 16th century before this miniature gazehound became readily available in southern Europe. The breed was admired for its beauty, small stature and loyalty. Many of these same fine

© Könemann Verlagsgesellschaft, mbH. Köln / A. Jemolo

qualities still are appreciated by millions of dog lovers around the world.

Today, the breed is most popular in the United States, Italy, England and

ANCIENT ANCESTORS

The Italian Greyhound is from very ancient lineage. The breed's ancestors were, in all likelihood, first known in Egypt, where they were depicted in many great works of art. There were paintings and carvings of tiny greyhound types on the walls of ancient Egyptian tombs.

Germany. However, Italian Greyhounds are also found in many other countries world-wide. During the Renaissance period, the breed was frequently included in family portraits and landscapes of that era. The paintings of Gerard David, Hans Memling, Lippi, Veronese and several others included the Italian Greyhound in numerous hunting scenes, religious art, statues and human portraits.

The Italian Greyhound carries an admirable heritage as the favorite of royalty and the privileged upper class. Even during ancient times, this loyal little sighthound was admired for its beauty, charm, elegance and entertaining disposition. The breed quickly became a favorite pet among Europe's royal families. Frederick the Great of Prussia, Queen Victoria, King Charles VIII, Anne of Denmark and Catherine the Great of Russia were just some of its famous supporters.

One interesting story of the Italian Greyhound concerns King or Chief Lobengula, the monarch of the Matabele, a warrior tribe of South Africa in the late 19th century. During a trip to Johannesburg, Lobengula noticed an Italian Greyhound owned by Luscombe Searelle. He was so fascinated by the high-stepping, prancing manner of the dog that he made an offer to purchase it. Initially, Searelle was unwilling to part with his cherished little friend. However, he quickly changed his mind when the monarch promised him 200 head of cattle in exchange for the dog.

Italian Greyhounds are currently competing successfully in all parts of the world in dog shows, obedience competitions, agility events and lure-coursing trials. In conformation, they have a growing accumulation of Best in Show awards to their credit. Despite years of life as a pet, the breed continues to hold on to its superb sighthound abilities.

The constant debate as to whether the breed should be classified as a lapdog or coursing hound still continues today. For

GENUS *CANIS*
Dogs and wolves are members of the genus *Canis*. Wolves are known scientifically as *Canis lupus* while dogs are known as *Canis domesticus*. Dogs and wolves are known to interbreed. The term "canine" derives from the Latin-derived word *Canis*. The term "dog" has no scientific basis but has been used for thousands of years. The origin of the word "dog" has never been authoritatively ascertained.

the most part, it appears that these exquisite miniature hounds possess qualities of both a loving companion and a diligent hunter of small game.

THE ITALIAN GREYHOUND IN ENGLAND

Over the last several hundred years, the Italian Greyhound has had a major influence in the UK. Many of the English nobility visited Italy during the late 18th and early 19th centuries and were intrigued by these small sighthounds. They frequently took the dogs back home with them as prized pets. Many of these commendable dogs became the foundation of some early British bloodlines.

Italian Greyhounds from the late 19th century, owned by British dog fancier, Mr. Anstice, who kept a kennel. These three champion dogs were sketched by R. H. Moore.

This male IG, Marco, was a consistent winner in the 1930s in the UK.

During the 19th century, the breed went through several changes in type and appearance. At this time, British Italian Greyhound fanciers were interested in producing tiny specimens of the breed. Many believed that producing smaller dogs would manifest better quality animals. In an effort to further reduce the breed's size, much inbreeding took place. This "fashionable" trend caused a complete deterioration of the breed in the UK. Poor dentition, deformed heads and large, bulging eyes were the end results of these poor breeding practices. In an effort to save and improve the breed, the first Italian

Greyhound Club of England was established in 1900. The club was interested solely in encouraging sound breeding programs and production of true type.

Today the UK is responsible for many of the dogs seen in America and other parts of the world. The foundation stock of many early American breeders originated in England, and there are several stud dogs of English descent that can be found in most of today's American pedigrees. Some of these top English dogs include Fleeting Flambeau of Cleden, Eng. Ch. Berinshill Dapper Dandy, Eng. Ch. Noways Matthew and Eng. Ch. Paolo of

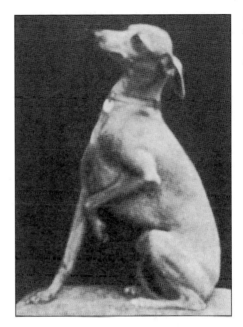

Isola Melinda, a 1932 favorite in Britain, was said to have originated in Italy or Turkey. She was bred by Clara Porter.

At the end of the 18th century, Italian Greyhounds were in great fashion and vied with the Pug for popularity.

A steel engraving of Italian Greyhounds, published in London in 1835, shown playing with ladies' possessions. The illustration emphasizes that these were dogs of high culture and prized by sophisticated female owners.

Myra, a popular dam in the early 1930s in Britain, shown with six of her puppies, many of which became champions. The litter was bred by Mrs. Mills of Worthing, England.

Chelstoncross. Some top influential English kennels include Berinshill, Bewick, Dairylane, Fleeting, Narrabo, Philtre, Tamoretta and Winterlea.

The Italian Greyhound was nearly decimated in England after World War I. However, after the war, English fanciers made a concerted effort to rebuild the breed. The effect of World War II on the dog world was almost identical to that of World War I; nearly all breeding activities came to an immediate halt. At this time, American breeders shipped some of their better stock to England. The Americans reintroduced some original English bloodlines that had been exported to the United States prior to the war's outbreak.

THE ITALIAN GREYHOUND IN THE UNITED STATES

According to the American Kennel Club (AKC) Stud Book, the Italian Greyhound was first

THE BREED AND THE RENAISSANCE

Although the breed has long been popular in the Mediterranean area, the breed did not acquire its name because it originated in Italy. The breed's association with Italian art during the Renaissance led to people's referring to the breed as the Italian Greyhound.

Isola Chloe was bred by Miss Porter in 1931 from an American bitch, Isola Princess.

LAPDOG AND SIGHTHOUND
In ancient times, Italian Greyhounds were originally intended to be lapdogs. However, they were frequently used for their superb sighthound and coursing abilities as they chased and captured small household vermin.

War I and II were culprits of the breed's decline and near-extinction. Governmental restrictions associated with both wars tremendously decreased breeding efforts.

The first Italian Greyhound shown in the US was at Gilmour's Garden in May 1877. By the mid-1900s, the breed began a slow but steady increase in popularity. However, it wasn't until 1954 that the Italian Greyhound Club of America was formed. Also in 1954, the first Italian Greyhound specialty was held at Rye, New York. Today the club consists of a membership of around 200 fanciers. The club is responsible for putting on yearly specialty shows, answering inquiries about the breed, promoting ethical breeding and providing other general information about Italian Greyhounds and the club's successful rescue scheme. Initially, a majority of the Italian Greyhound population in America was concentrated in the warmer parts of the country, such as

registered in the US in 1886. At this time, the breed's popularity was minimal and registrations in America were poor. Both World

Mary Hudson's Ch. Vogue's Truth or Dare Diamond, showing winning racing form.

Florida, Texas and California. As the breed's favorable qualities started to be recognized, its reputation spread throughout the country. Today the breed is represented in almost every part of the country. There are only a handful of dog shows where the breed is not well represented. Despite the breed's short coat, it has managed to adjust to colder climates quite well.

Over the years, the list of influential dogs and breeders has grown increasingly long. A few of the many influential kennels include Aira Vana, Bo-Bett, Candlewood, Dasa, Desertwind, Flagstone, Justa, L'Image, Littleluv, Marchwind, Mira, Pikop, Sandcastle, Silver Bluff, Starlite, Tekoneva, Tudor, Viva, Wildwind, Winsapphire and Zebec. These kennels have made a tremendous impression on the

Eng. Ch. Isola Sunshine, bred by Miss Porter in 1929, started winning in the same year and became a champion in 1932.

development and progress of the breed. They have combined to produce outstanding stud dogs, exceptional brood bitches and numerous top-winning champions.

In 1892, the Aira Vana kennel was established. Aira Vana is the oldest existing Italian Greyhound kennel in the United States. In 1949, the first Italian Greyhound to win the Toy Group was Aira Vana's Phillipi. In 1957, Porta's Westalica's Marcus became the first Italian Greyhound to earn his championship and an obedience title (Companion Dog, CD). The first Italian Greyhound to go Best in Show was Ch. Flaminia of Alpine in 1963.

"COUSIN" CONFUSION

The Italian Greyhound is frequently confused with its sighthound cousins, the Whippet and the Greyhound. The Italian Greyhound is at least one-third smaller than the Whippet, and nearly four or five times smaller than the Greyhound. The Italian Greyhound is a smaller and more delicate dog, but this should not discourage potential owners from keeping them. In fact, Italian Greyhounds are quite athletic and very capable of participating in many performance events.

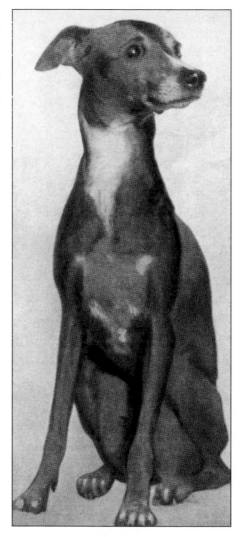

An Italian Greyhound, bred in Italy in the 1930s, originally published in *Hutchinson's Popular Dog Encyclopaedia*.

The first American Italian Greyhound magazine was established in 1959 by Helen Longshore and her daughter, Ann Hyres. Over the years, the magazine has increased in size and popularity and still remains the only true showcase for the breed in America. Subscribers to the publication can find useful articles about breed health issues and latest developments affecting the breed. In addition, there are advertisements and photographs of current top-winning dogs and breed ranking lists.

There are many fine Italian Greyhounds who have made their presence known through their offspring. Many dogs and pedigrees have become the backbone of the breed. Following is just a partial list of some of these top dogs: Ch. Dasa's King of the Mountain (bred by Richard and Patricia Sapp); Ch. Tekoneva's Dario (bred by Eva Partida and the top-winning Italian Greyhound male); Ch. Dasa's Ebony Queen; Ch. Flagstone Stock Option, CDX; Ch. Mira Latigo; Ch. Wavecrest Veni Vidi Vici and Ch. Winsapphire Joshua. At the end of the 20th century, the top-winning Italian Greyhound of all time in the show ring was a bitch named

FREDERICK THE GREAT

In the late 1700s, Frederick the Great of Prussia amassed quite a collection of Italian Greyhounds as his own cherished pets. Researchers believe that he may have had close to 40 Italian Greyhounds at one time. Frederick was so fond of the breed that some reports indicate that he carried his dogs with him into battle.

Ch. Donmar's Scarlet Ribbons.

The Italian Greyhound continues to be acknowledged by fanciers in America for its loyalty, kindness and ability to perform successfully in many different AKC-sanctioned events. Over the last 25 years, its popularity has increased dramatically, placing it in the top 50 AKC breeds.

Today, the Italian Greyhound continues to enjoy an increase in popularity outside England and America. Italy, Canada, Holland, Germany, France, Sweden and Australia are just some of the countries in which the breed has established a stronghold.

BABY OF THE FAMILY

The Italian Greyhound is the smallest of the family of sighthounds or gazehounds (dogs that hunt by sight). Despite their obvious hunting capabilities, there is no clear answer to the question of whether the breed was produced primarily as a companion dog or as a hunter. The breed is just as comfortable spending quality time indoors with its owner as it is chasing small vermin in the field.

A living, breathing artistic creation, the Italian Greyhound possesses style and grace that transcends the ages.

CHARACTERISTICS OF THE
ITALIAN GREYHOUND

TAKING CARE

Science is showing that as people take care of their pets, the pets are taking care of their owners. A recent study published in the *American Journal of Cardiology* found that having a pet can prolong his owner's life. Pet owners generally have lower blood pressure, and pets help their owners to relax and keep more physically fit. It was also found that pets help to keep the elderly connected to their communities.

IS THE ITALIAN GREYHOUND RIGHT FOR YOU?

Selecting a dog as your lifelong friend and companion is an exciting and satisfying experience. Dog ownership is a difficult and expensive commitment, which, when done properly, involves spending long hours training, nurturing and baby-sitting. Do you think you're up to the challenge?

If you've decided to add an Italian Greyhound to your life, you can be positive that you've made an excellent selection. The Italian Greyhound is a tremendously affectionate, long-lived, trustworthy and intelligent breed that is sure to provide you and your family with years of happiness and fun. An Italian Greyhound quickly bonds to his new owners, and once he's accepted you as his own, he will stand by your side throughout his lifetime. Italian Greyhounds do not eagerly accept the company of strangers or other unfamiliar people and faces, and it may take some time before they warm up to individuals they don't know. They will bark at strange noises and sounds, making them excellent watchdogs despite their small size. For intruders who can't see them, their bark is a lot bigger than their bite! Their small size makes them ideal for a life in a suburban or city setting. However, they do equally well and are just as content in the country or rural areas where they can have space to run and play. Regardless of your reasons for acquiring this elegant breed, you will quickly recognize that you could not have selected a better dog as a true loyal friend and companion.

The Italian Greyhound is a multi-purpose breed that serves as both a lapdog and a sighthound. They are happy either spending time indoors, curled under a warm blanket, or running wildly in the field, chasing small vermin. The breed was originally bred to keep the royal European families company and to chase small unwanted "house guests," such as field mice and small rats. They have tremendous stamina and athleticism for their size. If you like outdoor activities, you will find that the Italian Greyhound will enjoy spending free time participating in outdoor events or games.

They are surprisingly efficient little hunting dogs that have learned to adapt to changing weather conditions and climates. The breed's short coat allows them to fare much better in warmer and milder climates than in colder ones. However, they can

HEART HEALTHY
Over a decade ago, the *Australian Medical Journal* found that having pets is heart-healthy. Pet owners had lower blood pressure and lower levels of triglycerides than those who didn't have pets. It has also been found that senior citizens who own pets are more active and less likely to experience depression than those without pets.

adjust to colder climates and harsh winters if the change is brought on gradually. If it gets too cold or windy, many Italian Greyhound owners equip their dogs with small coats or sweaters.

Although not as popular as many other Toy breeds, the Italian Greyhound has attracted an ever-growing following in recent years. Most serious Italian Greyhounds breeders and enthusiasts don't

GREGARIOUS GREYHOUNDS
Italian Greyhounds interact well with one another, with dogs of different breeds and with other types of animals. They enjoy the company of other Italian Greyhounds and usually learn to accept each other from the onset. It's not uncommon for a group of them to sleep in pretzel-like fashion, stacked on top of each other like a pyramid.

mind that the breed is less common than many other sighthounds and Toy breeds. Thanks to a strong group of dedicated fanciers and breeders, the Italian Greyhound has not been exposed to some of the problems frequently associated with breed overpopulation. The limited demand for puppies has actually allowed the breed to remain very healthy and stable over the years.

Reputable breeders do their best to place puppies and dogs in homes that are well suited to the breed's personality and tempera-

ment. With this type of dog, this is not always easily accomplished. Adult Italian Greyhounds take extra time to adjust to new surroundings and people. New owners must be patient and allow adequate space and time for such changes.

The Italian Greyhound comes in a variety of interesting and striking colors. They are extremely intelligent dogs and loyal, rugged companions. Since the breed has a tremendous amount of stamina and energy, puppies can be challenging to train and discipline.

Italian Greyhounds are true family dogs that thrive on human interaction. At the same time, they can be quite reserved, even aloof, with strangers. They aren't very independent dogs and thoroughly enjoy the company of other Italian Greyhounds and other animals. They are true "people" dogs who enjoy the family setting and the companionship and attention of children. Since the breed is small and somewhat delicate, supervision and proper education is required for children who will be spending time with an Italian Greyhound.

It's important to remember that the Italian Greyhound is primarily a Toy breed and not a suitable pet for all interested individuals. They are very small and can "break" if handled too harshly. Broken limbs are unfortunately quite common in the breed, due to overly vigorous exercise or overzealous handling. Although they are very athletic, and fully capable of jumping and leaping great distances, they can easily be injured if allowed to roughhouse with children or larger, more aggressive dogs. Again, small children must always be carefully supervised while handling the breed under any circumstances, and must be taught to treat the dog with care and respect.

The Italian Greyhound does require a lot of training. However, they are quick learners and eager to please. Frequently, they are too smart for their own good! Their extreme intelligence can make them stubborn at times and difficult to work with. Patience is a virtue that must dwell in the homes of all Italian Greyhound owners. Keeping training interesting and challenging is one sure way to keep the breed's attention. They get bored easily and require new training objectives to keep them attentive and their minds sharp.

If a credible training approach is applied correctly, the Italian Greyhound will respond well to many methods of training. However, they can be sensitive at times and don't necessarily respond well to harsh corrections. The breed has been known to go to great lengths to deliberately test their owners' patience. Keeping

Although care must be taken with the IG's small limbs, the breed is surprisingly hardy and athletic— and definitely energetic!

them stimulated during training is one sure way to get them to cooperate and perform the different tasks that are asked of them. As with many other Toy breeds, house-training can be difficult, especially for male dogs.

PUPPY ENERGY

The Italian Greyhound puppy has an enormous amount of energy. It's well advised to keep the pup occupied with plenty of activities and under constant supervision. If you are planning to leave the pup alone at any time unsupervised, the puppy should be crated to keep him safe and out of trouble.

The versatility of the Italian Greyhound is widely recognized and proven. One of the great qualities of the Italian Greyhound is its ability to perform well in a multitude of activities. Their excellent coursing skills allow them to participate in different coursing events throughout the world. They also perform extremely well in agility trials, obedience events and flyball competitions. Furthermore, given the breed's elegant and natural showmanship, the Italian Greyhound is an excellent dog-show performer.

The breed's tiny size (ideally 13 to 15 inches in height) and fine bone structure are frequently misleading in that the general public believes the Italian Greyhound to be extremely delicate and frail. The truth is just the opposite. When cared for and conditioned properly, the breed is rather durable. The Italian Greyhound has great speed, nimbleness and athleticism. Italian Greyhounds need to be exercised regularly and should be allowed enough space to stretch their legs. Brisk 20-minute walks, three or four times a week, will keep them in excellent shape.

If you are looking for a dog that requires little grooming, the Italian Greyhound is ideal for you. The breed requires minimal grooming, which usually only involves basic bathing, nail trim-

ming, ear cleaning and brushing. Regular brushing is essential, especially after the dog exercises, to remove any loose dirt and to keep the coat shiny, healthy and in top condition.

Italian Greyhounds are found in a wide variety and combination of colors. They may be any color, but should not be brindle or have the black and tan markings found in other Toy breeds, such as the Miniature Pinscher or Toy Manchester Terrier. The breed's short, silk-like coat rarely sheds, which makes the breed ideal for potential owners with allergies or who simply don't want the trouble and responsibilities associated

Italian Greyhounds are very agile, fast and athletic, capable of competing in agility events and other areas of the dog sport.

with long-haired breeds.

Two of the most noteworthy physical characteristics of the breed are its movement and topline. The Italian Greyhound's movement is commonly misunderstood. The breed's movement should be high-stepping and free, with its front and hind legs moving forward in a straight line. A representative of the breed that moves properly should lift his front feet and have the ability to move forward with enough reach and drive, and cover enough ground for his size.

The Italian Greyhound's body should be of medium length, short-coupled and high at the

DO YOU WANT TO LIVE LONGER?
If you like to volunteer, it is wonderful if you can take your dog to a nursing home once a week for several hours. The elder community loves to have a dog with which to visit, and often your dog will bring a bit of companionship to someone who is lonely or somewhat detached from the world. You will be not only bringing happiness to someone else but also keeping your dog busy—and we haven't even mentioned the fact that it has been discovered that volunteering helps to increase your own longevity!

withers, with a curved back that droops at the hindquarters. However, despite these established recommended guidelines, many Italian Greyhounds competing in the show ring today have incorrect toplines that are exaggerated, roach-backed or wheel-backed. The ability to correctly interpret proper topline and movement has always been at the forefront of controversy in the breed.

HEALTH CONCERNS
Fortunately, the Italian Greyhound is a generally healthy breed; there are very few known hereditary problems. Nevertheless, there are some health

concerns of which every potential Italian Greyhound owner should be aware before acquiring the breed. PRA (progressive retinal atrophy), patellar subluxation, alopecia, dental problems and broken legs are not uncommon. It's imperative that pet owners, breeders and exhibitors make themselves aware of these potential health problems.

DENTAL PROBLEMS

Many Italian Greyhounds are born with poor dentition. If the teeth are not cleaned regularly (at least once a week), permanent tooth and gum damage can occur. It is not uncommon to see older dogs that are missing several teeth. Serious cases of gingivitis and periodontitis can destroy the teeth and, in more serious cases, the dog's internal organs. In some rare circumstances, the baby teeth of Italian Greyhounds need to be

Dental problems plague many Toy breeds, and the IG is no exception. Owners must commit to proper dental checkups and home care with their IGs to prevent their dogs from losing teeth at a young age.

removed by a qualified veterinarian if the teeth are retained for too long. Allowing the permanent teeth to emerge before the baby canines have fallen out can cause defective bites.

EYE PROBLEMS

Progressive retinal atrophy (PRA) is a serious genetic disorder that can cause blindness. The only way to be certain that your dog is not affected with the condition is to have him tested annually. Conscientious breeders have their breeding stock tested and certified by an eye specialist. You should do the same with your dog. Hopefully, in the very near future, veterinary researchers might be able to test for PRA genetic carriers in the IG.

Entropion is usually a congenital defect that involves the abnormal condition in which the eyelid rolls in toward the eye. Frequently, this condition causes the lashes to rub against the

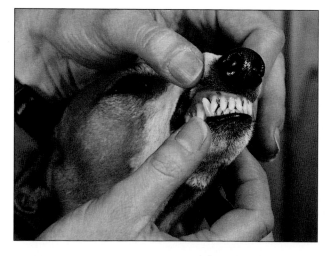

cornea and causes much irritation. Surgical correction is required to correct the problem.

Ectropion is the opposite of entropion. The lower eyelid rolls away from the eyeball. The condition is usually hereditary, but also can be caused by injury. Surgery can restore the eyelids to their proper location.

BLOAT

Bloat (gastric dilatation or torsion) is a serious condition that affects many breeds of dog. If a dog does not receive immediate medical aid when the condition occurs, they can easily die. Large, deep-chested dogs such as the Greyhound and Whippet are frequently affected, though any breed can be susceptible. A dog's stomach fills with gas, swells and twists, cutting off both entry and exit to the organ. The end result is death unless immediate veterinary treatment is administered by an experienced professional. Even then, there is no guarantee that a dog that is suffering from the ailment will recover. Causes of bloat include eating a large meal, drinking large quantities of water and exercising within two to three hours after or an hour before eating.

HYPOTHYROIDISM

Dogs that suffer from hypothyroidism lose hair on the flanks and back. In more serious cases,

GENDER SELECTION

Whether you choose to purchase a male or female Italian Greyhound is a matter of personal preference. However, many Italian Greyhound enthusiasts believe that the male dog is sometimes more difficult to house-train. The male Italian Greyhound is usually larger than the female, though the difference is quite inconsequential.

scaling and seborrhea are possible. Inadequate hormone levels are the cause of the condition. Fortunately, although many breeds suffer from hypothyroidism, the condition is easily treated with prescription medication from the veterinarian.

ALOPECIA

Alopecia (or baldness) is quite common in the Italian Greyhound. It can be caused by many different factors, including allergies, ment as soon as you suspect that the ailment might be present. Administering proper medication or even making small changes in a dog's diet can cure the problem.

BROKEN LEGS

A sometimes controversial subject among Italian Greyhound breed fanciers is broken legs. Despite what you may or may not have heard, leg breakage does occur. The Italian Greyhound is an active sighthound with long, skinny legs. Therefore, a young or adult dog can easily break a leg, or other bone for that matter, if allowed to jump from a high surface. A lot of broken legs occur because a dog is startled and moves suddenly. The incidence of leg breakage is higher in some bloodlines than in others. However, with a little common sense, a safe environment, a good balanced diet, proper exercise and conditioning, you can limit the chances of your dog's ever facing this problem.

SEIZURE DISORDERS

As in humans, seizures occur in Italian Greyhounds for many reasons. The disorder can be hereditary, can be caused by an allergic reaction or can be the result of poisoning, thyroid malfunction or hypoglycemia. Fortunately, once diagnosed, proper medication administered by a vet can usually correct the problem.

VETERINARY ATTENTION
Responsible Italian Greyhound owners must have an understanding of the medical problems associated with the breed. It's important that your dog receives regular physical examinations and be tested for genetic defects that occur in the breed.

hypothyroidism, hereditary conditions or some type of fungus infection. Italian Greyhounds that are blue in color suffer from this condition more frequently. However, alopecia can affect Italian Greyhounds of all colors. The condition usually occurs when a dog reaches two to three years of age. You should make an immediate trip to the vet for treat-

The elegant Artmeis Robins Rachel is an excellent example of the modern Italian Greyhound.

INTRODUCTION TO THE BREED STANDARD

A breed standard is an effort to define in words what the ideal physical specimen of a specified breed should look like. Although there will never be a "perfect" representative of any breed, it's significant to study and learn the standard. The standard is a valuable learning tool for both the novice and advanced dog fancier. If you learn to understand what your breed should look like and its original purpose, you can select a dog that is healthy and physically sound, and that is a worthy representative of the breed. Furthermore, your dog of choice will hopefully possess the distinct characteristics that you are looking for. Any reputable breeder should understand the breed standard and attempt to produce dogs that closely resemble it. If a breeder doesn't have the best interest of the breed in mind, you would be wise to look elsewhere for a dog.

Breed standards vary from kennel club to kennel club, from country to country. For the most part, each standard for a particular breed will describe the same

"ideal dog," though the terms, amount of detail and actual verbage vary. There are a few exceptions. Some colors are accepted in one standard and not in another, disqualifications exist in some standards and not in others, and so on. In addition, even the size requirements and bone structure of a breed may be altered from one standard to another. Be sure to check the standard for the country in which you live.

In theory, the dog that most closely "conforms" to the breed standard should be placed first in his class at a conformation show. Each show judge has his own interpretation of the standard, and he is expected to choose the dog that he feels is most representative of that breed on that given day. This is what makes competing in dog shows so exciting and enjoyable for all ages! Your dog's placement in a dog show can change from week to week, depending on the judge. The uncertainty and excitement are what keep thousands of exhibitors coming back weekend after weekend and year after year.

Do yourself a favor and learn

your breed standard. Study it well. It can only help you in the long run when the time comes to select a puppy, possibly begin a breeding program or even apply for a judge's license.

THE AMERICAN KENNEL CLUB STANDARD FOR THE ITALIAN GREYHOUND

Description: The Italian Greyhound is very similar to the Greyhound, but much smaller and more slender in all proportions and of ideal elegance and grace.

Head: Narrow and long, tapering to nose, with a slight suggestion of stop.

Skull: Rather long, almost flat.

Muzzle: Long and fine.

Nose: Dark. It may be black or brown or in keeping with the color of the dog. A light or partly pigmented nose is a fault.

Teeth: Scissors bite. A badly undershot or overshot mouth is a fault.

Eyes: Dark, bright, intelligent, medium in size. Very light eyes are a fault.

Ears: Small, fine in texture; thrown back and folded except when alerted, then carried folded

MEETING THE IDEAL
The American Kennel Club defines a standard as: "A description of the ideal dog of each recognized breed, to serve as an ideal against which dogs are judged at shows." This "blue-print" is drawn up by the breed's recognized parent club, approved by a majority of its membership and then submitted to the AKC for approval. The AKC states that "An understanding of any breed must begin with its standard. This applies to all dogs, not just those intended for showing." The picture that the standard draws of the dog's type, gait, temperament and structure is the guiding image used by breeders as they plan their programs.

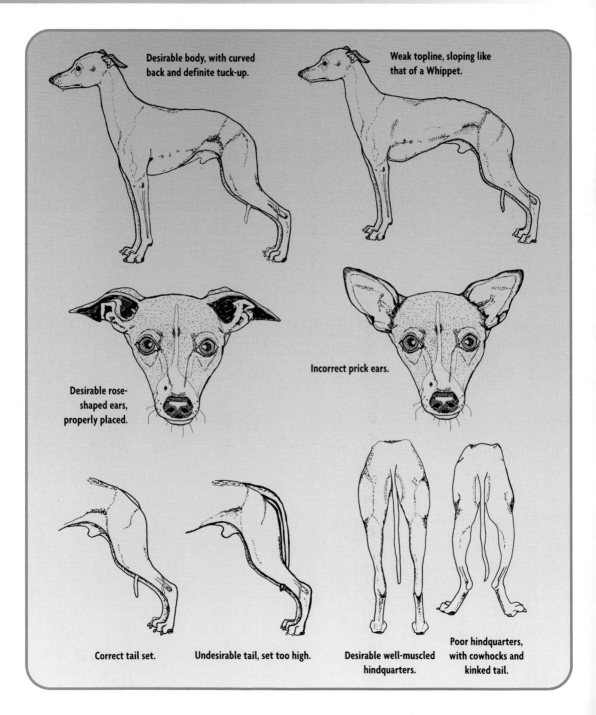

Desirable body, with curved back and definite tuck-up.

Weak topline, sloping like that of a Whippet.

Desirable rose-shaped ears, properly placed.

Incorrect prick ears.

Correct tail set.

Undesirable tail, set too high.

Desirable well-muscled hindquarters.

Poor hindquarters, with cowhocks and kinked tail.

at right angles to the head. Erect or button ears severely penalized.

Neck: Long, slender and gracefully arched.

Body: Of medium length, short coupled; high at withers, back curved and drooping at hindquarters, the highest point of curve at start of loin, creating a definite tuck-up at flanks.

Shoulders: Long and sloping.

Chest: Deep and narrow.

Forelegs: Long, straight, set well under shoulder; strong pasterns, fine bone.

Hindquarters: Long, well-muscled thigh; hind legs parallel when viewed from behind, hocks well let down, well-bent stifle.

Feet: Harefoot with well-arched toes. Removal of dewclaws optional.

Tail: Slender and tapering to a curved end, long enough to reach the hock; set low, carried low. Ring tail a serious fault, gay tail a fault.

Coat: Skin fine and supple, hair short, glossy like satin and soft to the touch.

Color: Any color and markings are

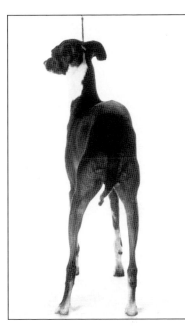

The hindquarters should be long and well muscled in the thighs, with legs parallel when viewed from behind.

acceptable except that a dog with brindle markings and a dog with the tan markings normally found on black-and-tan dogs of other breeds must be disqualified.

Action: High stepping and free, front and hind legs to move forward in a straight line.

Size: Height at withers, ideally 13 inches to 15 inches.

Disqualifications: A dog with brindle markings. A dog with the tan markings normally found on black-and-tan dogs of other breeds.

Approved December 14, 1976

ITALIAN GREYHOUND

LOCATING A BREEDER AND PUPPY

Finding a healthy and sound Italian Greyhound starts by contacting reputable breeders in your area. A good way to begin is to contact the American Kennel Club for referrals to the parent club and prospective breeders, or to visit a local dog show where the Italian Greyhound will be shown. Be prepared to do some driving.

Once you find a breeder with whom you feel comfortable, make arrangements to visit his kennel and meet his dogs. If there is a litter available, the puppies should be friendly and outgoing. If the litter's sire and dam are on the property (at least the dam should be), kindly ask to see them. Evaluate their appearance

Visiting a dog show and viewing the Italian Greyhound classes will give you the best possible idea of how quality dogs should appear.

and temperament, as they will be reflected in their offspring.

You must respect the opinions and suggestions of the breeder. Make it very clear as to what type of dog you are looking for. Are you looking for a pet? A show or breeding prospect? A male or female? An adult or puppy? Be prepared to answer questions about your own dog-caring experience. All responsible breeders are very careful about to whom they sell dogs. They are understandably concerned as to where the dogs from their kennel will be going and whether they will be cared for properly.

Once you have contacted and met a breeder or two and made your choice about which breeder is best suited to your needs, you will begin the puppy-picking process. Keep in mind that many top breeders have waiting lists. Sometimes new owners have to wait as long as a year, or even more, for a puppy from a particular line.

Since you are likely to be choosing an Italian Greyhound as a pet dog and not a show dog, you simply should select a pup that is friendly, attractive and healthy. Italian Greyhounds generally have small litters, averaging three puppies, so selection is limited once you have located a desirable litter. Always check the bite of your selected puppy to be sure that it is neither overshot nor under-shot. This may not be too notice-able on a young puppy, but will become more evident as the puppy gets older. You may also wish to check the bite of the puppy's sire and dam, if they are available for you to see, as dental problems can be an issue in the breed.

Some Italian Greyhounds have occasionally been criticized for being high-strung, shy, nerv-ous, aloof and even downright spooky. Some dogs produced from poor bloodlines may possess these undesirable quali-ties. However, poor temperament

ARE YOU PREPARED?
Unfortunately, when a puppy is bought by someone who does not take into consideration the time and attention that dog ownership requires, it is the puppy who suffers when he is either abandoned or placed in a shelter by a frustrated owner. So all of the "homework" you do in preparation for your pup's arrival will benefit you both. The more informed you are, the more you will know what to expect and the better equipped you will be to handle the ups and downs of raising a puppy. Hopefully, everyone in the household is willing to do his part in raising and caring for the pup. The anticipation of owning a dog often brings a lot of promises from excited family members: "I will walk him every day," "I will feed him," "I will house-train him," etc., but these things take time and effort, and promises can easily be forgotten once the novelty of the new pet has worn off.

"YOU BETTER SHOP AROUND!"

Finding a reputable breeder who sells healthy pups is very important, but make sure that the breeder you choose is not only someone you respect but also someone with whom you feel comfortable. Your breeder will be a resource long after you buy your puppy, and you must be able to call with reasonable questions without being made to feel like a pest! If you don't connect on a personal level, investigate some other breeders before making a final decision.

is more often the owner's fault for failing to adequately socialize the animal. There is no excuse for this type of behavior. Before purchasing an Italian Greyhound, or any type of dog, you must find one with a good temperament. Puppies that are eager for your attention and show no immediate signs of shyness or aggression are the types of dogs you should be considering for purchase.

Breeders commonly allow visitors to see their litters by around the fifth or sixth week, and puppies leave for their new homes around the tenth or twelfth week. Since Italian Greyhound puppies are so tiny, it is necessary for IG breeders to retain the pups longer than is necessary with most other breeds. Breeders who permit their puppies to leave early are more interested in your money than in their puppies' well-being. Puppies need to learn the rules of the pack from their dams, and most dams continue teaching the pups manners and dos and don'ts until the pups leave for new homes. Breeders spend significant amounts of time with the Italian Greyhound toddlers so that the pups are able to interact with the "other species," i.e., humans. Given the long history that dogs and humans have, bonding between the two species is natural but must be nurtured. A well-bred, well-socialized Italian Greyhound pup wants nothing more than to be near you and please you.

COMMITMENT OF OWNERSHIP

Researching your breed, selecting a responsible breeder and

observing as many pups as possible are all important steps on the way to dog ownership. It may seem like a lot of effort...and you have not even taken the pup home yet! Remember, though, you cannot be too careful when it comes to deciding on the type

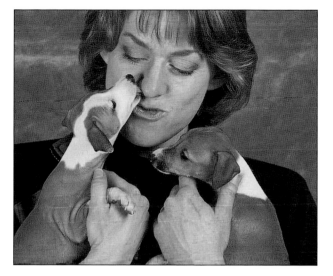

PEDIGREE VS. REGISTRATION CERTIFICATE

Too often new owners are confused between these two important documents. Your puppy's pedigree, essentially a family tree, is a written record of a dog's genealogy of three generations or more. The pedigree will show you the names as well as performance titles of all dogs in your pup's background. Your breeder must provide you with a registration application, with his part properly filled out. You must complete the application and send it to the AKC with the proper fee. Every puppy must come from a litter that has been AKC-registered by the breeder, born in the USA and from a sire and dam that are also registered with the AKC.

The seller must provide you with complete records to identify the puppy. The AKC requires that the seller provide the buyer with the following: breed; sex, color and markings; date of birth; litter number (when available); names and registration numbers of the parents; breeder's name; and date sold or delivered.

of dog you want and finding out about your prospective pup's background. Buying a puppy is not—or *should* not be—just another whimsical purchase. This is one instance in which you actually do get to choose your own family! You may be thinking that buying a puppy should be fun—it should not be so serious and so much work. Keep in mind that your puppy is not a cuddly stuffed toy or decorative ornament; rather, he is a living creature that will become a real member of your family. You will come to realize that, while buying a puppy is a pleasurable and exciting endeavor, it is not something to be taken lightly. Relax...the fun will start when the pup comes home!

Always keep in mind that a puppy is nothing more than a

The breeder should allow you to handle the puppies to see how they react to people and touching. Well-socialized puppies will enjoy being handled, though some pups may be more open with displays of affection.

ment of dog ownership. With some time and patience, it is really not too difficult to raise a curious and exuberant Italian Greyhound pup to be a well-adjusted and well-mannered adult dog—a dog that could be your most loyal friend.

PREPARING PUPPY'S PLACE IN YOUR HOME

Researching your breed and finding a breeder are only two aspects of the "homework" you will have to do before taking your Italian Greyhound puppy home. You will also have to prepare your home and family for the new addition. Much as you would prepare a nursery for a newborn baby, you will need to designate a place in your home that will be the puppy's own. How you prepare your home will depend on how much freedom the dog will be allowed. Whatever you decide, you must

By the time the puppies are ready for new homes, they should be completely weaned. IGs usually do not venture away from their dam until at least ten weeks of age, but weaning should be accomplished by the seventh or eighth week.

baby in a canine disguise…a baby who is virtually helpless in a human world and who trusts his owner for fulfillment of his basic needs for survival. In addition to food, water and shelter, your pup needs care, protection, guidance and love. If you are not prepared to commit to this, then you are not prepared to own a dog.

"Wait a minute," you say. "How hard could this be? All of my neighbors own dogs and they seem to be doing just fine. Why should I have to worry about all of this?" Well, you should not worry about it; in fact, you will probably find that once your Italian Greyhound pup gets used to his new home, he will fall into his place in the family quite naturally. However, it never hurts to emphasize the commit-

BOY OR GIRL?

An important consideration to be discussed is the sex of your puppy. For a family companion, a bitch may be the better choice, considering the female's inbred concern for all young creatures and her accompanying tolerance and patience. It is always advisable to spay a pet bitch or neuter a pet male, which may guarantee your IG a longer life.

ensure that he has a place that he can call his own.

When you bring your new puppy into your home, you are

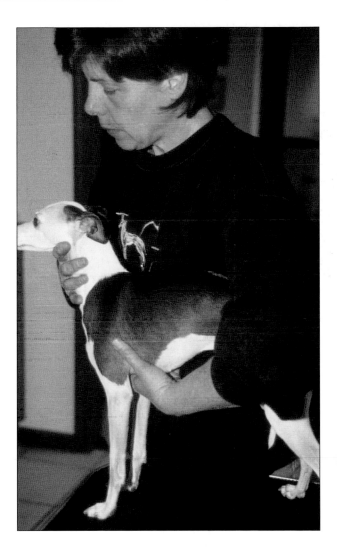

Owners will need to learn the proper way of lifting an IG. The IG should never be permitted to jump from a raised surface.

PUPPY APPEARANCE

Your puppy should have a well-fed appearance but not a distended abdomen, which may indicate worms or incorrect feeding, or both. The body should be firm, with a solid feel. The skin of the abdomen should be pale pink and clean, without signs of scratching or rash. Check the hind legs to see if the dewclaws were removed, if any were present at birth.

bringing him into what will become his home as well. Obviously, you did not buy a puppy with the intentions of catering to his every whim and allowing him to "rule the roost," but in order for a puppy to grow into a stable, well-adjusted dog,

PUPPY PERSONALITY

When a litter becomes available to you, choosing a pup out of all those adorable faces will not be an easy task! Sound temperament is of utmost importance, but each pup has his own personality and some may be better suited to you than others. A feisty, independent pup will do well in a home with older children and adults, while quiet, shy puppies will thrive in homes with minimal noise and distractions. Your breeder knows the pups best and should be able to guide you in the right direction.

he has to feel comfortable in his surroundings. Remember, he is leaving the warmth and security of his dam and littermates, as well as the familiarity of the only place he has ever known, so it is important to make his transition as easy as possible. By preparing a place in your home

for the puppy, you are making him feel as welcome as possible in a strange new place. It should not take him long to get used to it, but the sudden shock of being transplanted is somewhat traumatic for a young pup. Imagine how a small child would feel in the same situation—that is how your puppy must be feeling. It is up to you to reassure him and to let him know, "Little guy, you are going to like it here!"

WHAT YOU SHOULD BUY

CRATE

To someone unfamiliar with the use of crates in dog training, it may seem like punishment to shut a dog in a crate, but this is not the case at all. Most breeders advocate crate training for show dogs and pet dogs alike.

Crates are not cruel—crates

Breeders often expose their litters to crates so that the pups are not fearful when they encounter one. This litter looks perfectly content checking out the crate that has been provided.

YOUR SCHEDULE . . .
If you lead an erratic, unpredictable life, with daily or weekly changes in your work requirements, consider the problems of owning a puppy. The new puppy has to be fed regularly, socialized (loved, petted, handled, introduced to other people) and, most importantly, allowed to go outdoors for house-training. As the dog gets older, he can be more tolerant of deviations in his feeding and relief schedule.

PHOTO COURTESY OF DOSKOCIL

soft bedding and his favorite toy, a crate becomes a cozy pseudo-den for your dog. Like his ancestors, he too will seek out the comfort and retreat of a den—you just happen to be providing him with something a little more luxurious than what his early ancestors enjoyed.

As far as purchasing a crate, the type that you buy is up to you. It will most likely be one of the two most popular types: wire or fiberglass. There are advantages and disadvantages to each type. For example, a wire crate is more open, allowing the air to

have many humane and highly effective uses in dog care and training. For example, crate training is a very popular and very successful house-training method. In addition, a crate can keep your dog safe during travel and, perhaps most importantly, a crate provides your dog with a place of his own in your home. It serves as a "doggie bedroom" of sorts—your Italian Greyhound can curl up in his crate when he wants to sleep or when he just needs a break. Many dogs sleep in their crates overnight. With

CRATE-TRAINING TIPS

During crate training, you should partition off the section of the crate in which the pup stays. If he is given too big an area, this will hinder your training efforts. Crate training is based on the fact that a dog does not like to soil his sleeping quarters, so it is ineffective to keep a pup in an area that is so big that he can eliminate in one end and get far enough away from it to sleep. Also, you want to make the crate den-like for the pup. Blankets and a favorite toy will make the crate cozy for the small pup; as he grows, you may want to evict some of his "roommates" to make more room. It will take some coaxing at first, but be patient. Given some time to get used to it, your pup will adapt to his new home-within-a-home quite nicely.

flow through and affording the dog a view of what is going on around him, while a fiberglass crate is sturdier. Both can double as travel crates, providing protection for the dog in the car. Purchase a small crate for your Italian Greyhound, and it should suffice for the puppy and fully-grown dog as well.

BEDDING

A soft pad in the dog's crate will help the dog feel more at home, and you may also like to give him a small blanket. First, these things will take the place of the leaves, twigs, etc., that the pup would use in the wild to make a den; the pup can make his own "burrow" in the crate. Although your pup is far removed from his den-making ancestors, the denning instinct is still a part of his genetic makeup. Second, until you take your pup home, he has been sleeping amid the warmth of his dam and litter-mates, and while a blanket is not the same as a warm, breathing body, it still provides heat and something with which to snuggle. You will want to wash your pup's bedding frequently in case he has a toileting accident in his crate, and replace or remove any blanket or padding that becomes ragged and starts to fall apart.

TOYS

Toys are a must for dogs of all ages, especially for curious playful pups. Puppies are the "children" of the dog world, and what child does not love toys? Safe chew toys provide enjoyment for both dog and owner—your dog will enjoy playing with his favorite toys, while you will enjoy the fact that they distract him from chewing on your expensive shoes and leather sofa. Puppies love to chew; in fact,

A room with a view, ideally an Italian landscape, is preferred: wire crates afford the IG better visibility of his surroundings as well as good ventilation.

TOYS, TOYS, TOYS!

With a big variety of dog toys available, and so many that look like they would be a lot of fun for a dog, be careful in your selection. It is amazing what a set of puppy teeth can do to an innocent-looking toy, so, obviously, safety is a major consideration. Be sure to choose the most durable products that you can find. Hard nylon bones and toys are a safe bet, and many of them are offered in different scents and flavors that will be sure to capture your dog's attention. It is always fun to play a game of fetch with your dog, and there are balls and flying discs that are specially made to withstand dog teeth.

chewing is a physical need for pups as they are teething, and everything looks appetizing! The full range of your possessions—from slippers to Oriental carpet—are fair game in the eyes of a teething pup. Puppies are not all that discerning when it comes to finding something literally to "sink their teeth into"—everything tastes great!

Provide your Italian Greyhound with safe, durable toys; only those made specifically for dogs. Breeders advise owners to resist stuffed toys, because they can become de-stuffed in no time. The overly excited pup may ingest the stuffing, which is neither digestible nor nutritious. Similarly, squeaky toys are quite popular, but must be avoided for the Italian Greyhound. Perhaps a squeaky toy can be used as an aid in training, but not for free play. If a pup "disembowels" one of these, the small plastic squeaker inside can be danger-ous if swallowed. Monitor the condition of all your pup's toys carefully and get rid of any that have been chewed to the point of becoming potentially dangerous.

Be careful of natural bones, which have a tendency to splin-ter into sharp, dangerous pieces. Also be careful of rawhide, which can turn into pieces that are easy to swallow or become a mushy mess on your carpet.

MENTAL AND DENTAL

Toys not only help your puppy get the physical and mental stimulation he needs but also provide a great way to keep his teeth clean. Hard rubber or nylon toys, especially those constructed with grooves, are designed to scrape away plaque, preventing bad breath and gum infection. Strong rope toys act like floss as the dog chews.

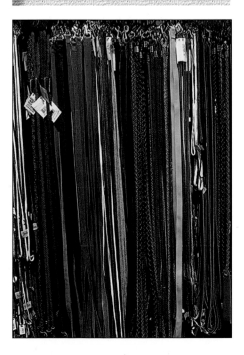

LEAD

A nylon lead is probably the best option, as it is the most resistant to puppy teeth should your pup take a liking to chewing on his lead. Of course, this is a habit that should be nipped in the bud, but, if your pup likes to chew on his lead, he has a very slim chance of being able to chew through the strong nylon. Nylon leads are also lightweight, which is good for a young Italian Greyhound who is just getting used to the idea of walking on a lead. For everyday walking and safety purposes, the nylon lead is a good choice.

As your pup grows up and gets used to walking on the lead, you may want to purchase a flexible lead. These leads allow you to extend the length to give the dog a broader area to explore or to shorten the length to keep the dog near you.

Adults and puppies alike love to play with fun toys. Make sure all of your IG's toys are safe and made especially for dogs.

Select a light yet strong nylon lead for your IG from the wide selection available at most pet-supply stores.

CHOOSE AN APPROPRIATE COLLAR

The **BUCKLE COLLAR** is the standard collar used for everyday purposes. Be sure that you adjust the buckle on growing puppies. Check it every day. It can become too tight overnight! These collars can be made of leather or nylon. Attach your dog's identification tags to this collar.

The **CHOKE COLLAR** is designed for training. It is constructed of highly polished steel so that it slides easily through the stainless steel loop. The idea is that the dog controls the pressure around his neck and he will stop pulling if the collar becomes uncomfortable. It is not suitable for use on the Italian Greyhound.

The **HALTER** is for a trained dog that has to be restrained to prevent running away, chasing a cat and the like. Considered the most humane of all collars, it is frequently used on smaller dogs on which collars are not comfortable.

COLLAR

Your pup should get used to wearing a collar all the time since you will want to attach his ID tags to it; plus, you have to attach the lead to something! A lightweight nylon collar is a good choice. Make certain that the collar fits snugly enough so that the pup cannot wriggle out of it, but is loose enough so that it will not be uncomfortably tight around the pup's neck. You should be able to fit a finger or two between the pup's neck and the collar. It may take some time for your pup to get used to wearing the collar, but soon he will not even notice that it is there. Choke collars are made for training, but should not be used on small dogs like the Italian Greyhound.

FOOD AND WATER BOWLS

Your pup will need two bowls, one for food and one for water. You may want two sets of bowls, one for indoors and one for outdoors, depending on where the dog will be fed and where he will be spending time. Stainless steel or sturdy plastic bowls are popular choices. Plastic bowls are more chewable, but dogs tend not to chew on the steel variety, which can be sterilized. It is important to buy sturdy bowls since anything is in danger of being chewed by puppy teeth and you do not want

FINANCIAL RESPONSIBILITY
Grooming tools, collars, leashes, a crate, a dog bed and, of course, toys will be expenses to you when you first obtain your pup, and the cost will continue throughout your dog's lifetime. If your puppy damages or destroys your possessions (as most puppies surely will!) or something belonging to a neighbor, you can calculate additional expense. There is also flea and pest control, which every dog owner faces more than once. You must be able to handle the financial responsibility of owning a dog.

Your local pet shop sells an array of bowls for water and food. Your may wish to elevate your IG's bowls on stands to create a more natural feeding position and aid his digestion.

PHOTO COURTESY OF MIKKI PET PRODUCTS.

your dog to be constantly chewing apart his bowl (for his safety and for your wallet!).

CLEANING SUPPLIES

Until a pup is house-trained, you will be doing a lot of cleaning. "Accidents" will occur, which is acceptable in the beginning stages of house-training because the puppy does not know any better. All you can do is be prepared to clean up any accidents as soon as they happen. Old rags, towels, newspapers and a safe disinfectant are good to have on hand.

BEYOND THE BASICS

The items previously discussed are the bare necessities. You will find out what else you need as you go along—grooming supplies, flea/tick protection, baby gates to partition a room, etc. These things will vary depending on your situation, but it is important that right away

you have everything you need to feed and make your Italian Greyhound comfortable in his first few days at home.

PUPPY-PROOFING YOUR HOME
Aside from making sure that your Italian Greyhound will be comfortable in your home, you also have to make sure that your home is safe for your Italian Greyhound. This means taking precautions that your pup will not get into anything he should not get into and that there is nothing within his reach that may harm him should he sniff it, chew it, inspect it, etc. This

probably seems obvious since, while you are primarily concerned with your pup's safety, at the same time you do not want your belongings to be ruined. Breakables should be placed out of reach if your dog is to have full run of the house. If he is to be limited to certain places within the house, keep any potentially dangerous items

It is your responsibility to clean up after your dog has relieved himself. Pet shops have various aids to assist in the cleanup job.

SKULL & CROSSBONES
Thoroughly dog-proof your house before bringing your IG home. Never use cockroach or rodent poisons or plant fertilizers in any area accessible to the dog. Avoid the use of toilet cleaners. Most dogs are born with "toilet-bowl sonar" and will take a drink if the lid is left open. Also keep the trash secured and out of reach. IGs are naturally curious throughout wheir lives and will investigate the unknown, so always ensure a safe environment.

NATURAL TOXINS

Examine your grass and landscaping before bringing your puppy home. Many varieties of plants have leaves, stems or flowers that are toxic if ingested, and you can depend on a curious puppy to investigate them. Ask your vet for information on poisonous plants or research them at your library.

If you see your dog carrying a piece of vegetation in his mouth, approach him in a quiet, disinterested manner, avoid eye contact, pet him and gradually remove the plant from his mouth. Alternatively, offer him a treat and maybe he'll drop the plant on his own accord. Be sure no toxic plants are growing in your own yard or kept in your home.

IGs have little problem plotting to steal food or other tasty items from counter-tops. Keep a close eye on your IG and do not leave food or breakable items where your dog can reach them.

make a great chew toy? Cords should be fastened tightly against the wall. If your dog is going to spend time in a crate, make sure that there is nothing near his crate that he can reach if he sticks his curious little nose or paws through the openings. Just as you would with a child, keep all household cleaners and chemicals where the pup cannot reach them; antifreeze is especially dangerous to dogs.

It is also important to make sure that the outside of your home is safe. Of course, your puppy should never be unsuper-

in the "off-limits" areas.

An electrical cord can pose a danger should the puppy decide to taste it—and who is going to convince a pup that it would not

HOW VACCINES WORK

If you've just bought a puppy, you surely know the importance of having your pup vaccinated, but do you understand how vaccines work? Vaccines contain the same bacteria or viruses that cause the disease you want to prevent, but they have been chemically modified so that they don't cause any harm. Instead, the vaccine causes your dog to produce antibodies that fight the harmful bacteria. Thus, if your dog is exposed to the disease in the future, the antibodies will destroy the viruses or bacteria.

vised, but a pup let loose in the yard will want to run and explore, and he should be granted that freedom. Do not let a fence give you a false sense of security; you would be surprised at how crafty (and persistent) a dog can be in working out how to dig under and squeeze his way through small holes, or to jump or climb over a fence. The remedy is to make the fence well embedded into the ground and high enough so that it really is impossible for your dog to get over it (about 5 feet should suffice). Be sure to secure any gaps in the fence, since a determined Italian Greyhound can easily squeeze through a very tiny hole. Check the fence peri-

odically to ensure that it is in good shape and make repairs as needed; a very determined pup may return to the same spot to "work on it" until he is able to get through.

FIRST TRIP TO THE VET

You have selected your puppy, and your home and family are ready. Now all you have to do is collect your Italian Greyhound from the breeder and the fun begins, right? Well...not so fast. Something else you need to plan is your pup's first trip to the veterinarian. Perhaps the breeder can recommend someone in your area who specializes in sighthounds or Toy breeds, or maybe you know some other Italian Greyhound owners who can suggest a good vet. Either way, you should have an appointment arranged for your pup before you pick him up.

The pup's first visit will consist of an overall examination

Although he looks like a work of art, your IG won't be as still as a statue when there's exploring to do!

Your IG pup may be a bit apprehensive on his first day in your home. Offer him all the comforts of home without overwhelming him. He will adjust at his own pace.

to make sure that the pup does not have any problems that are not apparent to you. The veterinarian will also set up a schedule for the pup's vaccinations; the breeder will inform you of which ones the pup has already received and the vet can continue from there.

INTRODUCTION TO THE FAMILY

Everyone in the house will be excited about the puppy's coming home and will want to pet him and play with him, but it is best to keep the introductions low-key so as not to overwhelm the puppy. He is apprehensive already. It is the first time he has been separated from his dam and the breeder, and the ride to your home is likely to be the first time he has been in a car. The last thing you want to do is smother him, as this will only frighten him further. This is not to say that human contact is not extremely necessary at this stage, because this is the time when a connection between the pup and his human family is formed. Gentle petting and soothing words should help console him, as well as just putting him down and letting him explore on his own (under your watchful eye, of course).

The pup may approach the family members or may busy himself with exploring for a while. Gradually, each person should spend some time with the pup, one at a time, crouching down to get as close to the pup's level as possible while letting him sniff their hands and petting him gently. He definitely needs human attention and he needs to be touched—this is how to form an immediate bond. Just remember that the pup is experiencing many things for the first time, at the same time. There are new people, new noises, new smells and new things to investigate, so be gentle, be affectionate and be as comforting as you can be.

PUP'S FIRST NIGHT HOME

You have traveled home with your new charge safely in his crate. He's been to the vet for a thorough check-up; he's been weighed, his papers have been examined and perhaps he's even been vaccinated and wormed as well. He's met the whole family, including the excited children and the less-than-happy cat. He's explored his area, his new bed, the yard and anywhere else he's been permitted. He's eaten his first meal at home and relieved himself in the proper place. He's heard lots of new sounds, smelled new friends and seen more of the outside world than ever before...and that was just the first day! He's worn out and is ready for bed...or so you think!

It's puppy's first night home and you are ready to say "Good night." Keep in mind that this is his first night ever to be sleeping alone. His dam and littermates are no longer at paw's length and he's a bit scared, cold and lonely.

Be reassuring to your new family member, but this is not the time to spoil him and give in to his inevitable whining.

Puppies whine. They whine to let others know where they are and hopefully to get company out of it. Place your pup in his new bed or crate in his designated area and close the door. Mercifully, he may fall

FEEDING TIPS

You will probably start feeding your pup the same food that he has been getting from the breeder; the breeder should give you a few days' supply to start you off. Although you should not give your pup too many treats, you will want to have puppy treats on hand for coaxing, training, rewards, etc. Be careful, though, as a small pup's calorie requirements are relatively low and a few treats can add up to almost a full day's worth of calories without the required nutrition.

IN DUE TIME

It will take at least two weeks for your puppy to become accustomed to his new surroundings. Give him lots of love, attention, handling, frequent opportunities to relieve himself, a diet he likes to eat and a place he can call his own.

asleep without a peep. When the inevitable occurs, however, ignore the whining—he is fine. Be strong and keep his interest in mind. Do not allow yourself to feel guilty and visit the pup. He will fall asleep eventually.

Many breeders recommend placing a piece of bedding from the pup's former home in his new bed so that he recognizes and is comforted by the scent of his littermates. Others still advise placing a hot water bottle in the bed for warmth. The latter may be a good idea, provided the pup doesn't attempt to suckle— he'll get good and wet, and may not fall asleep so fast.

Puppy's first night can be somewhat stressful for both the pup and his new family. Remember that you are setting the tone of nighttime at your house. Unless you want to play with your pup every night at 10 p.m., midnight and 2 a.m., don't initiate the habit. Your family will thank you, and so will your pup!

PREVENTING PUPPY PROBLEMS

SOCIALIZATION

Now that you have done all of the preparatory work and have helped your pup get accustomed to his new home and family, it is about time for you to have some fun! Socializing your Italian Greyhound pup gives you the opportunity to show off your new friend, and your pup gets to reap the benefits of being an adorable and intriguing creature that people will want to pet and, in general, think is absolutely precious!

Besides getting to know his new family, your puppy should be exposed to other people, animals and situations. This will help him become well adjusted as he grows up and less prone to being timid or fearful of the new things he will encounter. Of course, he must not come into close contact with dogs you don't know well until his course of injections is fully complete.

Your pup's socialization began with the breeder, but now it is your responsibility to continue it. The socialization he receives in the first few weeks after coming home is the most critical, as this is the time when he forms his impressions of the outside world. From eight to ten weeks of age, puppies experience what is known as the "fear period." Your IG pup will still be at the breeder's at this age, and the interaction he receives during this time should be gentle and reassuring. Lack of socialization, and/or negative experiences

PUP MEETS WORLD

Thorough socialization includes not only meeting new people but also being introduced to new experiences such as riding in the car, having his coat brushed, hearing the television, walking in a crowd—the list is endless. The more your pup experiences, and the more positive the experiences are, the less of a shock and the less frightening it will be for your pup to encounter new things.

during the socialization period, can manifest itself in fear and aggression as the dog grows up. Your puppy needs lots of positive interaction, which of course includes human contact, affection, handling and exposure to other animals.

Once your pup has received his necessary vaccinations, feel free to take him out and about (on his lead, of course). Walk him around the neighborhood, take him on your daily errands, let people pet him, let him meet other dogs and pets, etc. Puppies do not have to try to make friends; there will be no shortage of people who will want to introduce themselves. Just make sure

For the safety of your IG, supervise any interaction between the dog and the family cat. A cat's sharp claws and teeth can do regrettable damage to the feisty IG!

and pups most often make great companions. However, sometimes an excited child can unintentionally handle a pup too roughly, or an overzealous pup can playfully nip a little too hard. You want to make socialization experiences positive ones. What a pup learns during this very formative stage will affect his attitude toward future encounters. You want your dog to be comfortable around everyone. A pup that has a bad experience with a child may grow up to be a dog that is shy around or aggressive toward children.

MANNERS MATTER

During the socialization process, a puppy should meet people, experience different environments and definitely be exposed to other canines. Through playing and interacting with other dogs, your puppy will learn lessons, ranging from controlling the pressure of his jaws by biting his littermates to the inner-workings of the canine pack that he will apply to his human relationships for the rest of his life. That is why removing a puppy from the litter too early can be detrimental to the pup's development.

that you carefully supervise each meeting. If the neighborhood children want to say hello, for example, that is great—children

CONSISTENCY IN TRAINING

Dogs, being pack animals, naturally need a leader, or else they try to establish dominance in their packs. When you welcome a dog into your family, the choice of who becomes the leader and who becomes the "pack" is entirely up to you! Your pup's intuitive quest for dominance, coupled with the fact that it is nearly impossible to look at an adorable Italian Greyhound pup, with his inquisitive expression and his "puppy-dog" eyes, and not cave in, give the pup almost an unfair advan-

TOXIC TREATS

Chocolate contains the chemical thebromine, which is poisonous to dogs, although "chocolates" especially made for dogs are safe (as they don't actually contain chocolate) but not recommended. Any item that encourages your dog to enjoy the taste of cocoa should be discouraged. You should also exercise caution when using mulch in your garden. This frequently contains cocoa hulls, and dogs have been known to die from eating the mulch. Onions are another "people food" toxic to dogs. Remember, even a very small amount of a toxic substance can poison the tiny IG.

Italian Greyhounds, when properly trained, make delightful, obedient pets for caring owners. The breed has been prized for its devotion and gentle nature for centuries.

tage in getting the upper hand!

A pup will definitely test the waters to see what he can and cannot do. Do not give in to those pleading eyes—stand your ground when it comes to disciplining the pup and make sure that all family members do the same. It will only confuse the pup if Mother tells him to get out of the bedroom when he is used to resting there with Father to watch the nightly news. Avoid discrepancies by having all members of the household decide on the rules before the pup even comes home…and be consistent in enforcing them! Early training shapes the dog's personality, so you cannot be unclear in what you expect.

COMMON PUPPY PROBLEMS

The best way to prevent puppy problems is to be proactive in stopping an undesirable behavior as soon as it starts. The old saying "You can't teach an old dog new tricks" does not necessarily hold true, but it *is* true that it is much easier to discourage bad behavior in a young developing pup than to wait until the pup's bad behavior

becomes the adult dog's bad habit. There are some problems that are especially prevalent in puppies as they develop.

NIPPING

As puppies start to teethe, they feel the need to sink their teeth into anything available…unfortunately, that usually includes your fingers, arms, hair and toes. You may find this behavior cute for the first five seconds…until you feel just how sharp those puppy teeth are. Nipping is something you want to discourage immediately and consistently with a firm "No!" (or whatever number of firm "Nos" it takes for him to understand that you mean business). Then, replace your finger with an appropriate chew toy. While this behavior is merely annoying when the dog is young, it can become dangerous as your Italian Greyhound's adult teeth grow in and his jaws develop if he continues to think it is okay to nibble on his human friends. Your Italian Greyhound does not mean any harm with a friendly nip, but he also does not know his own strength.

CRYING/WHINING

Your pup will often cry, whine, whimper, howl or make some type of commotion when he is left alone. This is basically his way of calling out for attention to make sure that you know he is there

TRAINING TIP

Training your IG takes much patience and can be frustrating at times, but you should see results from your efforts. If you have a puppy that seems untrainable, take him to a trainer or behaviorist. The dog may have a personality problem that requires the help of a professional, or perhaps you need help in learning how to train your dog.

and that you have not forgotten about him. Your puppy feels insecure when he is left alone, when you are out of the house and he is in his crate or when you are in another part of the house and he cannot see you. The noise he is making is an expression of the anxiety he feels at being alone, so he needs to be taught that being alone is okay. You are not actually training the dog to stop making noise; rather, you are training him to feel comfortable when he is alone and thus removing the need for him to make the noise.

This is where the crate with cozy bedding and a toy comes in handy. You want to know that your pup is safe when you are not there to supervise, and you know that he will be safe in his crate rather than roaming freely about the house. In order for the pup to stay in his crate without making a fuss, he first needs to be comfortable in his crate. On that note, it is extremely important that the crate is never used as a form of punishment; this will cause the pup to view the crate as a negative place, rather than as a place of his own for safety and retreat.

Accustom the pup to the crate in short, gradually increasing time intervals in which you put him in the crate, maybe with a treat, and stay in the room with him. If he cries or makes a fuss, do not go to him, but stay in his sight. Gradually he will realize that

CHEWING TIPS

Chewing goes hand in hand with nipping in the sense that a teething puppy is always looking for a way to soothe his aching gums. In this case, instead of chewing on you, he may have taken a liking to your favorite shoe or something else that he should not be chewing. Again, realize that this is a normal canine behavior that does not need to be discouraged, only redirected. Your pup just needs to be taught what is acceptable to chew on and what is off-limits. Consistently tell him "No!" when you catch him chewing on something forbidden and give him a chew toy.

Conversely, praise him when you catch him chewing on something appropriate. In this way, you are discouraging the inappropriate behavior and reinforcing the desired behavior. The puppy's chewing should stop after his adult teeth have come in, but an adult dog continues to chew for various reasons—perhaps because he is bored, needs to relieve tension or just likes to chew. That is why it is important to redirect his chewing when he is still young.

staying in his crate is just fine without your help, and it will not be so traumatic for him when you are not around. You may want to leave the radio on softly when you leave the house; the sound of human voices may be comforting to him.

DIETARY AND FEEDING CONSIDERATIONS

Today the choices of food for your Italian Greyhound are many and varied. There are simply dozens of brands of food in all sorts of flavors and textures, ranging from puppy diets to those for seniors. There are even hypoallergenic and low-calorie diets available. Because your Italian Greyhound's food has a bearing on coat, health and temperament, it is essential that the most suitable diet is selected for a Italian Greyhound of his age. It is fair to say, however, that even experienced owners can be perplexed by the enormous range of foods available. Only understanding what is best for your dog will help you reach an informed decision.

Dog foods are produced in three basic types: dry, semi-moist and canned. Dry foods are useful for the cost-conscious, for overall they tend to be less expensive than semi-moist or canned foods. Dry foods also contain the least fat and the most preservatives. In general, canned foods are made up of 60–70% water, while semi-moist ones often contain so much sugar that they are perhaps the least preferred by owners, even though their dogs seem to like them.

STORING DOG FOOD
You must store your dry dog food carefully. Open packages of dog food quickly lose their vitamin value, usually within 90 days of being opened. Mold spores and vermin could also contaminate the food.

When selecting your dog's diet, three stages of development must be considered: the puppy stage, the adult stage and the senior stage.

PUPPY STAGE

Puppies instinctively want to suck milk from their mother's teats; a normal puppy will exhibit this behavior just a few moments following birth. If puppies do not attempt to suckle within the first half-hour or so, they should be encouraged to do so by placing them on the nipples, having selected ones with plenty of milk. This early milk supply is important in providing the essential colostrum, which protects the puppies during the first eight to ten weeks of their lives. Although a mother's milk is much better than any milk formula, despite there being some excellent ones available, if the puppies do not feed, the breeder will have to feed them by hand. For those with less experience, advice from a veterinarian is important so that not only the right quantity of milk is fed but also that of correct quality, fed at suitably frequent intervals, usually every two hours during the first few days of life.

Puppies should be allowed to nurse from their mothers for about the first six weeks, although, starting around the

FOOD PREFERENCE

Selecting the best dry dog food is difficult. There is no majority consensus among veterinary scientists as to the value of nutrient analysis (protein, fat, fiber, moisture, ash, cholesterol, minerals, etc.). All agree that feeding trials are what matter most, but you also have to consider the individual dog. The dog's weight, age and activity level, and what pleases his taste, all must be considered. It is probably best to take the advice of your veterinarian. Every dog has individual dietary requirements, and should be fed accordingly.

If your dog is fed a good dry food, he does not require supplements of meat or vegetables. Dogs do appreciate a little variety in their diets, so you may choose to stay with the same brand but vary the flavor. Alternatively, you may wish to add a little flavored stock to give a difference to the taste.

There is no better food for the puppy than mother's milk. The puppy should be completely weaned by the time he is seven to eight weeks old.

FEEDING TIPS

- Dog food must be served at room temperature, neither too hot nor too cold. Fresh water, changed often and served in a clean bowl, is mandatory.
- Never feed your dog from the table while you are eating, and never feed your dog leftovers from your own meal. They usually contain too much fat and too much seasoning.
- Dogs must chew their food. Hard pellets are excellent; soups and stews are to be avoided.
- Don't add leftovers or any extras to commercial dog food. The normal food is usually balanced, and adding something extra destroys the balance.
- Except for age-related changes, dogs do not require dietary variations. They can be fed the same diet, day after day, without their becoming bored or ill.

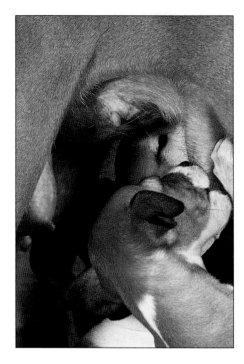

third or fourth week, the breeder will begin to introduce small portions of suitable solid food. Most breeders like to introduce alternate milk and meat meals initially, building up to weaning time.

By the time the puppies are seven or a maximum of eight weeks old, they should be fully weaned and fed solely on a proprietary puppy food. Selection of the most suitable, good-quality diet at this time is essential, for a puppy's fastest growth rate is during the first year of life. Your breeder and vet will be able to offer advice in this regard. The frequency of meals will be reduced over time as the puppy grows and, when a young dog has reached the age of about 12 months, an adult diet can be fed. Puppy and junior diets should be well balanced for the needs of your dog so that, except in certain circumstances, additional vitamins, minerals and proteins will not be required.

ADULT DIETS

A dog is considered an adult when he has stopped growing, so in general the diet of an Italian Greyhound can be changed to an adult one at about 12 months of age. An Italian Greyhound is fully mature around 12 months of age, though it often takes another 12 to 18 months for dog to reach his peak as a show dog. Again you should rely upon your veterinarian or dietary specialist to recommend an acceptable maintenance diet. Major dog-food manufacturers specialize in this type of food, and it is merely necessary for you to select the one best suited to your dog's needs. Active dogs may have different requirements than sedentary dogs.

SENIOR DIETS

As dogs get older, their metabolism changes. The older dog usually exercises less, moves more slowly and sleeps more. This change in lifestyle and

TIPPING THE SCALES

Good nutrition is vital to your dog's health, but many people end up over-feeding or giving unnecessary supplements. Here are some common doggie diet don'ts:

- Adding milk, yogurt and cheese to your dog's diet may seem like a good idea for coat and skin care, but dairy products are very fattening and can cause indigestion.
- Diets high in fat will not cause heart attacks in dogs but will certainly cause your dog to gain weight.
- Most importantly, don't assume your dog will simply stop eating once he doesn't need any more food. Given the chance, he will eat you out of house and home!

physiological performance requires a change in diet. Since these changes take place slowly, they might not be recognizable. What is easily recognizable is weight gain. By continuing to feed your dog an adult-maintenance diet when he is slowing

The puppy does not eat "dog food," he eats "puppy food." Discuss the best brand with your breeder. Follow his advice regarding how much to feed and how often.

down metabolically, your dog will gain weight. Obesity in an older dog compounds the health problems that already accompany old age. Extra weight will

GRAIN-BASED DIETS

Some less expensive dog foods are based on grains and other plant proteins. While these products may appear to be attractively priced, many breeders prefer a diet based on animal proteins and believe that they are more conducive to your dog's health. Many grain-based diets rely on soy protein, which may cause flatulence (passing gas).

There are many cases, however, when your dog might require a special diet. These special requirements should only be recommended by your veterinarian.

put stress on the Italian Greyhound's delicate bones.

As your dog gets older, few of his organs function up to par. The kidneys slow down and the intestines become less efficient. These age-related factors are best handled with a change in diet and a change in feeding schedule to give smaller portions that are more easily digested. There is no single best diet for every older dog. While many dogs do well on light or senior diets, other dogs do better on puppy diets or special premium diets such as lamb and rice. Be sensitive to your senior Italian Greyhound's diet, as this will help control other problems that may arise with your old friend.

WATER

Just as your dog needs proper nutrition from his food, water is an essential "nutrient" as well.

Water keeps the dog's body properly hydrated and promotes normal function of the body's systems. During house-training, it is necessary to keep an eye on how much water and when your Italian Greyhound is drinking, but, once he is reliably trained, he should have free access to clean fresh water at all times, especially if you feed dry food. Make certain that the dog's water bowl is clean, and change the water often.

EXERCISE

All dogs require some form of exercise, regardless of breed. A sedentary lifestyle is as harmful to a dog as it is to a person. The Italian Greyhound is an active breed that enjoys exercise, but you don't have to be an Olympic athlete to provide your dog with a sufficient amount of activity! Exercising your Italian Greyhound can be enjoyable and healthy for both of you. Brisk walks, once the puppy reaches three or four months of age, will stimulate heart rates and build muscle for both dog and owner. As the dog reaches adulthood, the speed and distance of the walks can be increased as long as they are kept reasonable and comfortable for both of you. Since the Italian Greyhound's legs are so small, the owner's idea of a "long walk" may be different from the perception of

"DOES THIS COLLAR MAKE ME LOOK FAT?"

While humans may obsess about how they look and how trim their bodies are, many people believe that extra weight on their dogs is a good thing. The truth is, pets should not be over- or under-weight, as both can lead to or signal sickness. In order to tell how fit your pet is, run your hands over his ribs. Are his ribs buried under a layer of fat or are they sticking out considerably? If your pet is within his normal weight range, you should be able to feel the ribs easily, but they should not protrude abnormally. If you stand above him, the outline of his body should resemble an hourglass. The IG is a lean breed that should not carry excess weight. Making sure your dog is the right weight for his breed will certainly contribute to his good health.

If properly socialized, your IG and cat can be trusted together, though sharing a food bowl is not a wise option for any owner.

DRINK, DRANK, DRUNK— MAKE IT A DOUBLE

In both humans and dogs, as well as other living organisms, water forms the major part of nearly every body tissue. Naturally, we take water for granted, but without it, life as we know it would cease.

For dogs, water is needed to keep their bodies functioning biochemically. Additionally, water is needed to replace the water lost while panting. Unlike humans, who are able to sweat to dissipate heat, dogs must pant to cool down, thereby losing the vital water that their bodies need to regulate their body temperatures. Humans lose electrolyte-containing products and other body-fluid components through sweating; dogs do not lose anything except water.

Water is essential always, but especially so when the weather is hot or humid or when your dog is exercising or working vigorously.

his miniature friend! A couple of blocks, never more than a mile, is all that is necessary for the Italian Greyhound, perhaps three or four times weekly.

Play sessions in the yard and letting the dog run free in the yard under your supervision also are sufficient forms of exercise for the Italian Greyhound. Fetching games can be played indoors or out; these are excellent for giving your dog active play that he will enjoy. Chasing things that move comes naturally to dogs of all breeds, especially alert sighthounds. When your Italian Greyhound runs after the ball or object, praise him for picking it up and encourage him to bring it back to you for another throw. Never go to the object and pick it up yourself, or you'll soon find that you are the one retrieving the objects rather than the dog! If you choose to play games outdoors, you must have a securely fenced-in yard and/or have the dog attached to at least a 25-foot light line for security. You want your Italian Greyhound to run, but not run away!

Bear in mind that an overweight dog should never be suddenly over-exercised; instead, he should be encouraged to increase exercise slowly. Also remember that not only is exercise essential to keep the dog's body fit, it is essential to his

A Worthy Investment

Veterinary studies have proven that a balanced high-quality diet pays off in your dog's coat quality, behavior and activity level. Invest in premium brands for the maximum payoff with your dog.

your dog. Many dogs grow to like the feel of being brushed and will enjoy the routine.

BATHING

Dogs do not need to be bathed as often as humans, but bathing as needed is important for healthy skin and a clean, shiny coat. Again, like most anything, if you accustom your IG to being bathed as a puppy, it will be second nature by the time he grows up. You want your dog to be at ease in the bath or else it

mental well-being. A bored dog will find something to do, which often manifests itself in some type of destructive behavior. In this sense, exercise is just as essential for the owner's mental well-being!

GROOMING THE ITALIAN GREYHOUND

BRUSHING

A natural bristle brush or a hound glove can be used for regular routine brushing. Regular once-overs are effective for removing dead hair and stimulating the dog's natural oils to add shine and a healthy look to the coat. Although the Italian Greyhound's coat is short and close, it does require a five-minute once-over to keep it looking its shiny best. Regular grooming sessions are also a good way to spend time with

THAT'S ENTERTAINMENT!

Is your dog home alone for much of the day? If you haven't taught him how to crochet or play the French horn, then he'll probably need something to occupy his paws and jaws, lest he turn to chewing the carpet. Recommended conditioning devices are toys that stimulate your dog both physically and mentally. Some of the most popular toys are those that are constructed to hide food inside. They provide not only a challenge but also instant gratification when your dog gets to the treat. Be sure to clean these carefully to prevent bacteria from building up.

GROOMING EQUIPMENT

How much grooming equipment you purchase will depend on how much grooming you are going to do. Here are some basics:

- Natural bristle brush
- Hound glove
- Flea comb
- Rubber mat
- Dog shampoo
- Spray hose attachment
- Towels
- Ear cleaner
- Cotton balls
- Nail clippers
- Dental-care products

you are washing the rest of his body. You should use only a shampoo that is made for dogs. Do not use a product made for human hair. Work the shampoo all the way down to the skin. You can use this opportunity to check the skin for any bumps, bites or other abnormalities. Do not neglect any area of the body—get all of the hard-to-reach places.

Once the dog has been thoroughly shampooed, he requires an equally thorough rinsing. Shampoo left in the coat can be irritating to the dog's skin. Protect his eyes from the shampoo by shielding them with your

A natural bristle brush or a hound glove is ideal for the Italian Greyhound's short, sleek coat.

could end up a wet, soapy, messy ordeal for both of you!

Give your Italian Greyhound a quick once-over before wetting his coat. This will get rid of any dead hair, dirt or dust in the coat. Make certain that your dog has a good non-slip surface on which to stand. Begin by wetting the dog's coat, checking the water temperature to make sure that it is neither too hot nor too cold. A shower or hose attachment is necessary for thoroughly wetting and rinsing the coat.

Next, apply shampoo to the dog's coat and work it into a good lather. Wash the head last, as you do not want shampoo to drip into the dog's eyes while

The Italian Greyhound needs little grooming. Your local pet shop will have a wide variety of grooming tools from which you can select the tools best suited to your needs.

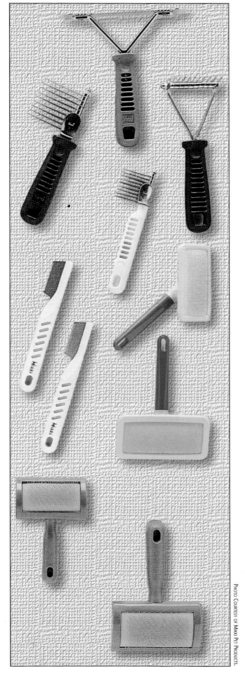

SOAP IT UP

The use of human soap products like shampoo, bubble bath and hand soap can be damaging to a dog's coat and skin. Human products are too strong; they remove the protective oils coating the dog's hair and skin that make him water-resistant. Use only shampoo made especially for dogs. You may like to use a medicated shampoo, which will help to keep external parasites at bay.

hand and directing the flow of water in the opposite direction. You should also avoid getting water in the ear canal. Be prepared for your dog to shake out his coat—you might want to stand back, but make sure you have a hold on the dog to keep him from running through the house, and have a towel ready.

EAR CLEANING

The ears should be kept clean with a cotton ball or pad and and ear-cleaning product made

PHOTO COURTESY OF MIKKI PET PRODUCTS.

BATHING BEAUTY
Once you are sure that the dog is thoroughly rinsed, squeeze the excess water out of his coat with your hand and dry him with a heavy towel. You may choose to use a blow dryer, on very low heat, on his coat or just let it dry naturally. In cold weather, never allow your dog outside with a wet coat.

There are "dry bath" products on the market, which are sprays and powders intended for spot cleaning, that can be used between regular baths if necessary. They are not substitutes for regular baths, but they are easy to use for touch-ups as they do not require rinsing.

especially for dogs. Do not probe into the ear canal with anything, as this can cause injury. Be on the lookout for any signs of infection or ear-mite infestation. If your Italian Greyhound has been shaking his head or scratching at his ears frequently, this usually indicates a problem. If the dog's ears have an unusual odor, this is a sure sign of mite infestation or infection, and a signal to have his ears checked by the vet.

NAIL CLIPPING
Your Italian Greyhound should be accustomed to having his nails trimmed at an early age since nail clipping will be part of your maintenance routine throughout his life. Not only does it look nicer, but long nails can scratch someone unintentionally. Also, a long nail has a better chance of ripping and bleeding, or causing the feet to spread. A good rule of thumb is that if you can hear your dog's nails clicking on the floor when he walks, his nails are too long.

Before you start cutting, make sure you can identify the "quick" in each nail. The quick is a blood vessel that runs through the center of each nail and grows rather close to the end. The quick will bleed if accidentally cut, which will be quite painful for the dog as it contains nerve endings. Keep some type of clotting agent on hand, such as a styptic pencil or styptic powder (the type used for shaving). This will stop the bleeding quickly when applied to the end of the cut nail. Do not panic if you cut the quick, just stop the bleeding and talk soothingly to your dog. Once he has calmed down, move on to the next nail. It is better to clip a little at a time, particularly with dark nails.

Hold your pup steady as you begin trimming his nails; you do not want him to make any sudden movements or run away. Talk to him soothingly and stroke him as you clip. Holding his foot in your hand, simply

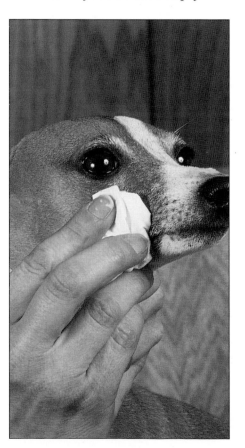

Tear stains can be gently removed with preparations sold in pet shops.

PEDICURE TIP

A dog that spends a lot of time outside on a hard surface, such as cement or pavement, will have his nails naturally worn down and may not need to have them trimmed as often, except maybe in the colder months when he is not outside as much. Regardless, it is best to get your dog accustomed to the nail-trimming procedure at an early age so that he is used to it. Some dogs are especially sensitive about having their feet touched, but if a dog has experienced it since puppyhood, it should not bother him.

take off the end of each nail with one swift clip. You should purchase nail clippers that are made for use on dogs; you can probably find them wherever you buy grooming supplies.

Do not poke anything into the dog's ear canal. The ears should be kept clean with a cotton ball and canine ear powder, rather than with a cotton swab, which can be dangerous if it enters the ear canal.

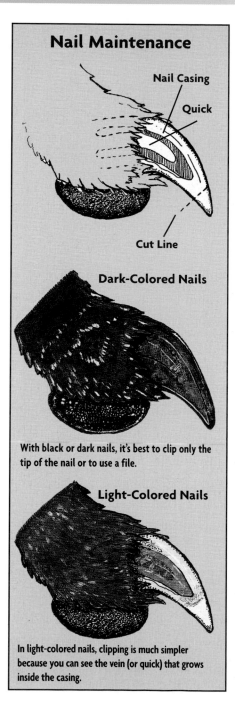

Nail Maintenance

Nail Casing

Quick

Cut Line

Dark-Colored Nails

With black or dark nails, it's best to clip only the tip of the nail or to use a file.

Light-Colored Nails

In light-colored nails, clipping is much simpler because you can see the vein (or quick) that grows inside the casing.

TRAVELING WITH YOUR DOG

CAR TRAVEL

You should accustom your Italian Greyhound to riding in a car at an early age. You may or may not take him in the car often, but at the very least he will need to go to the vet and you do not want these trips to be traumatic for the dog or troublesome for you. The safest way for a dog to ride in the car is in his crate. If he uses a crate in the house, you can use the same crate for travel.

Put the pup in the crate and see how he reacts. If he seems uneasy, you can have a passenger hold him on his lap while you drive. Another option for very small dogs is a ventilated "carrying case," which resembles a duffel bag and can be held on a passenger's lap. Do not let the dog roam loose in the vehicle—this is very dangerous! If you should stop short, your dog can be thrown and injured. If the dog starts climbing on you and pestering you while you are driving, you will not be able to concentrate on the road. It is an unsafe situation for everyone—human and canine.

For long trips, bring along some water for the dog be prepared to stop to let him relieve himself. Always keep your IG on lead when you make stops. Take with you whatever

Your IG's crate is the safest place for him to be during car rides. Never allow the dog to be unrestrained in a moving vehicle.

TRAVEL ALERT
When you travel with your dog, it's a good idea to take along water from home or to buy bottled water for the trip. In areas where water is sometimes chemically treated and sometimes comes right out of the ground, you can prevent adverse reactions to this essential part of your dog's diet.

you need to clean up after him, including some paper towels and perhaps some old rags for use should he have a potty accident in the car or suffer from motion sickness.

It's important to remember to never leave your dog alone in the car, not even for a few minutes. In hot weather, your Italian Greyhound can die from the high temperature inside a closed vehicle; even a car parked in the shade can heat up very quickly. Leaving the window open is dangerous as well since the dog can hurt himself trying to get out.

AIR TRAVEL WITH YOUR IG
Contact your chosen airline before proceeding with your travel plans that include your IG. The dog will be required to travel in a fiberglass crate and you should always check in advance with the airline regarding specific requirements. To help put the dog at ease, give him one of his favorite toys in the crate. Do not feed the dog for several hours before the trip in order to minimize his need to relieve himself; a light meal is best. Make sure your dog is properly identified and that your contact information appears on his ID tags and on his crate.

Discuss with your chosen airline whether or not your IG can travel as a "carry-on." Many airlines offer this privilege to small-dog owners so that the dog can remain in the cabin with his owner. The crate must be able to fit under the passenger's seat. If the airline doesn't permit this kind of travel, keep trying until you find one that will give your IG "first-class" treatment.

VACATIONS AND BOARDING

So you want to take a family vacation—and you want to include *all* members of the family. You would probably make arrangements for accommodations ahead of time anyway, but this is especially important when traveling with a dog. You do not want to make an overnight stop at the only place around for miles, only to find out that they do not allow dogs. Also, you do not want to reserve a place for your family without confirming that you are traveling with a dog, because, if it is against their policy, you may end up without a place to stay.

Alternatively, if you are traveling and choose not to bring your Italian Greyhound, you will have to make arrangements for

Owners may have to reconsider their holiday plans if their senior IG is no longer apt to travel.

HOMESITTING

Another option for the traveling dog owner is the homesitter. These unique organizations are comprised of bonded individuals who will stay at your home to look after your pet and property while you are away.

You will be fortunate to find a reliable boarding facility that can house small dogs. Never leave your IG in a kennel with which you are not completely comfortable.

him while you are away. Some options are to take him to a friend's house to stay while you are gone, to have a trusted friend stay at your house or to bring your dog to a reputable boarding kennel. If you choose to board him at a kennel, you should visit in advance to see the facilities provided and where the dogs are kept. Are the dogs' areas appropriately sized and kept clean? Is this an ideal facility for such a small dog? Talk to some of the employees and see how they handle the dogs—do they spend time with the dogs, play with them, exercise them, etc.? Also find out the kennel's policy on vaccinations and what they require. This is for all of the dogs' safety, since there is a greater risk of diseases being passed from dog to dog when dogs are kept together.

CONSIDERATIONS ABOUT BOARDING

Will your dog be exercised at least twice a day? How often during the day will the staff keep him company? Does the kennel provide a clean and secure environment? These are some of the questions you should consider when choosing a boarding kennel.

Likewise, if the staff asks you a lot of questions, this is a good sign. They need to know your dog's personality and temperament, health record, special requirements and what commands he has learned. Above all, follow your instincts. If you have a bad feeling about a kennel, even if a friend has recommended it, don't put your dog in that kennel's care.

IDENTIFICATION

Your Italian Greyhound is your valued companion and friend. That is why you always keep a close eye on him and you have made sure that he cannot escape from the yard or wriggle out of his collar and run away from you. However, accidents can happen and there may come a time when your dog unexpectedly becomes separated from you. If this unfortunate event should occur, the first thing on your mind will be finding him. Proper identification, including an ID tag and perhaps a tattoo and/or a microchip, will increase the chances of his being returned to you safely and quickly.

IDENTIFICATION OPTIONS

As puppies become more and more expensive, especially those puppies of high quality for showing and/or breeding, they have a greater chance of being stolen. The usual collar dog tag is, of course, easily removed. But there are two more permanent techniques that have become widely used for identification.

The puppy microchip implantation involves the injection of a small microchip, about the size of a corn kernel, under the skin of the dog. If your dog shows up at a clinic or shelter, or is offered for resale under less-than-savory circumstances, he can be positively identified by the microchip. The microchip is scanned, and a registry quickly identifies you as the owner.

Tattooing is done on various parts of the dog, from his belly to his ears. The number tattooed can be your telephone number, your dog's registration number or any other number that you can easily memorize. When professional dog thieves see a tattooed dog, they usually lose interest. For the safety of our dogs, no laboratory facility or dog broker will accept a tattooed dog as stock.

Discuss microchipping and tattooing with your veterinarian and breeder. Some vets perform these services on their own premises for a reasonable fee. To ensure that your dog's identification is effective, be certain that the dog is then properly registered with a legitimate national database.

Since you value your IG, you must take steps ensure his safety.

TRAINING YOUR

ITALIAN GREYHOUND

Living with an untrained dog is a lot like owning a piano that you do not know how to play—it is a nice object to look at, but it does not do much more than that to bring you pleasure. Now try taking piano lessons, and suddenly the piano comes alive and brings forth magical sounds and rhythms that set your heart singing and your body swaying.

REAP THE REWARDS
If you start with a normal, healthy dog and give him time, patience and some carefully executed lessons, you will reap the rewards of that training for the life of the dog. And what a life it will be! The two of you will find immeasurable pleasure in the companionship you have built together with love, respect and understanding.

The same is true with your Italian Greyhound. Any dog—no matter how small—is a big responsibility and, if not trained sensibly, may develop unacceptable behavior that annoys you or could even cause family friction.

To train your Italian Greyhound, you may like to enroll in an obedience class. Teach your dog good manners as you learn how and why he behaves the way he does. Find out how to communicate with your dog and how to recognize and understand his communications with you. Suddenly the dog takes on a new role in your life—he is clever, interesting, well behaved and fun to be with. He demonstrates his bond of devotion to you daily. In other words, your Italian Greyhound does wonders for your ego because he constantly reminds you that you are not only his leader, you are his hero!

Those involved with teaching dog obedience and counseling owners about their dogs' behavior have discovered some interesting facts about dog ownership. For example, training dogs when they are puppies results in the highest rate of success in developing well-mannered and well-adjusted adult dogs. Training an older dog, from six months to six years of age, can produce almost equal results, providing that the owner accepts the dog's slower rate of learning capability and is willing to work patiently to help the dog succeed at developing to his fullest potential. Unfortunately, many owners of untrained adult dogs lack the patience factor, so they do not persist until their dogs are successful at learning particular behaviors.

Training a puppy aged 10 to 16 weeks (20 weeks at the most) is like working with a dry sponge in a pool of water. The

HONOR AND OBEY

Dogs are the most honorable animals in existence. They consider another species (humans) as their own. They interface with you. You are their leader. Puppies perceive children to be on their level; their actions around small children are different from their behavior around their adult masters.

pup soaks up whatever you show him and constantly looks for more things to do and learn. At this early age, his body is not yet producing hormones, and therein lies the reason for such a high rate of success. Without hormones, he is focused on his owners and not particularly interested in investigating other places, dogs, people, etc. You are his leader: his provider of food, water, shelter and security. He latches onto you and wants to stay close. He will usually follow you from room to room, will not let you out of his sight when you are outdoors with him and will respond in like manner

Training two dogs presents a double challenge if they distract each other. You want the dogs to focus on you and the lesson at hand, and playtime can come later!

Puppyhood is the time when you make an impression on your young IG and set the tone for your role as his pack leader for his entire life.

to the people and animals you encounter. If you greet a friend warmly, he will be happy to greet the person as well. If, however, you are hesitant or anxious about the approach of a stranger, he will respond accordingly.

Once the puppy begins to produce hormones, his natural curiosity emerges and he begins to investigate the world around him. It is at this time when you may notice that the untrained dog begins to wander away from you and even ignore your commands to stay close. When this behavior becomes a problem, you have two choices: get rid of the dog or train him. It is strongly urged that you choose the latter option.

You usually will be able to find obedience classes within a reasonable distance from your home, but you can also do a lot

to train your dog yourself. Sometimes there are classes available, but the tuition is too costly. Whatever the circumstances, the solution to training your dog without formal obedience classes lies within the pages of this book.

This chapter is devoted to helping you train your Italian Greyhound at home. If the recommended procedures are followed faithfully, you may expect positive results that will prove rewarding both to you and your dog.

Whether your new charge is a puppy or a mature adult, the methods of teaching and the techniques we use in training basic behaviors are the same. After all, no dog, whether puppy or adult, likes harsh or inhumane methods. All creatures, however, respond favorably to gentle motivational methods and sincere praise and encouragement. Now let us get started.

PARENTAL GUIDANCE
Training a dog is a life experience. Many parents admit that much of what they know about raising children they learned from caring for their dogs. Dogs respond to love, fairness and guidance, just as children do. Become a good dog owner and you may become an even better parent.

CANINE DEVELOPMENT SCHEDULE

It is important to understand how and at what age a puppy develops into adulthood. If you are a puppy owner, consult the following Canine Development Schedule to determine the stage of development your puppy is currently experiencing. This knowledge will help you as you work with the puppy in the weeks and months ahead.

Period	Age	Characteristics
FIRST TO THIRD	**BIRTH TO SEVEN WEEKS**	Puppy needs food, sleep and warmth, and responds to simple and gentle touching. Needs mother for security and disciplining. Needs littermates for learning and interacting with other dogs. Pup learns to function within a pack and learns pack order of dominance. Begin socializing pup with adults and children for short periods. Pup begins to become aware of his environment.
FOURTH	**EIGHT TO TWELVE WEEKS**	Brain is fully developed. Pup needs socializing with outside world. Remove from mother and littermates. Needs to change from canine pack to human pack. Human dominance necessary. Fear period occurs between 8 and 12 weeks. Avoid fright and pain.
FIFTH	**THIRTEEN TO SIXTEEN WEEKS**	Training and formal obedience should begin. Less association with other dogs, more with people, places, situations. Period will pass easily if you remember this is pup's change-to-adolescence time. Be firm and fair. Flight instinct prominent. Permissiveness and over-disciplining can do permanent damage. Praise for good behavior.
JUVENILE	**FOUR TO EIGHT MONTHS**	Another fear period about 7 to 8 months of age. It passes quickly, but be cautious of fright and pain. Sexual maturity reached. Dominant traits established. Dog should understand sit, down, come and stay by now.

NOTE: THESE ARE APPROXIMATE TIME FRAMES. ALLOW FOR INDIVIDUAL DIFFERENCES IN PUPPIES.

IGs are sensitive, intelligent dogs that never respond to harsh training methods. To train an IG, you must be positive and encouraging.

cult for both dog and owner.

Next, choose the command you will use each and every time you want your puppy to void. "Hurry up" and "Let's go" are examples of commands commonly used by dog owners. Get in the habit of giving the puppy your chosen relief command before you take him out. That way, when he becomes an adult, you will be able to determine if he wants to go out when you ask him. A confirmation will be signs of interest, such as wagging his tail, watching you intently, going to the door, etc.

PUPPY'S NEEDS
The puppy needs to relieve himself after play periods, after each meal, after he has been sleeping and at any time he indicates that he is looking for a place to urinate or defecate. The urinary and intestinal tract muscles of very young puppies

HOUSE-TRAINING
You can train a puppy to relieve himself wherever you choose, but this must be somewhere suitable. You should bear in mind from the outset that when your puppy is old enough to go out in public places, any canine deposits must be removed at once. You will always have to carry with you a small plastic bag or "poop-scoop."

Outdoor training includes such surfaces as grass, soil and cement. Indoor training usually means training your dog to newspaper. When deciding on the surface and location that you will want your Italian Greyhound to use, be sure it is going to be permanent. Training your dog to grass and then changing your mind a few months later is extremely diffi-

CALM DOWN
Dogs will do anything for your attention. If you reward the dog when he is calm and attentive, you will develop a well-mannered dog. If, on the other hand, you greet your dog excitedly and encourage him to wrestle with you, the dog will greet you the same way and you will have a hyperactive dog on your hands.

TAKE THE LEAD

Do not carry your dog to his relief area. Lead him there on a leash or, better yet, encourage him to follow you to the spot. If you start carrying him to his spot, you might end up doing this routine forever and your dog will have the satisfaction of having trained *you*.

too much for him to handle. Instead, offer the puppy clearly defined areas where he can play, sleep, eat and live. A room of the house where the family gathers is the most obvious choice. Puppies are social animals and need to feel a part of the pack right from the start. Hearing your voice, watching you while you are doing things and smelling you nearby are all positive reinforcers that he is now a member of your pack. Usually a family room, the kitchen or a

are not fully developed. Therefore, like human babies, puppies need to relieve themselves frequently.

Take your puppy out often—every hour when he first comes home, for example—and always immediately after sleeping and eating. The older the puppy, the less often he will need to relieve himself. Finally, as a mature healthy adult, he will require only three to five relief trips per day.

HOUSING

Since the types of housing and control you provide for your puppy have a direct relationship on the success of house-training, we consider the various aspects of both before we begin training.

Taking a new puppy home and turning him loose in your house can be compared to turning a child loose in a sports arena and telling the child that the place is all his! The sheer enormity of the place would be

Once your IG is house-trained, you can provide him with his own access to the backyard. You can't expect a puppy to figure this out, but a grown dog loves to come and "go" as he pleases.

MEALTIME

Mealtime should be a peaceful time for your IG. Do not put his food and water bowls in a high-traffic area in the house. For example, give him his own little corner of the kitchen where he can eat undisturbed and where he will not be underfoot. Do not allow small children or other family members to disturb the dog when he is eating.

nearby adjoining breakfast area is ideal for providing safety and security for both puppy and owner.

Within the designated room, there should be a smaller area that the puppy can call his own. An alcove, a wire or fiberglass dog crate or a gated corner from which he can view the activities of his new family will be fine. The size of the area or crate is the key factor here. The area must be large enough so that the puppy can lie down and stretch out, as well as stand up, without rubbing his head on the top. At the same time, it must be small enough so that he cannot relieve himself at one end and sleep at the other without coming into contact with his droppings. Dogs are, by nature, clean animals and will not remain close to their relief areas unless forced to do so. In those cases, they then become dirty dogs and usually remain that way for life.

The dog's designated area should contain clean bedding and a toy. Water must always be available, in a non-spill container, although you will want to monitor your pup's water intake during house-training so you can predict when he will need to go out.

CONTROL

By *control*, we mean helping the puppy to create a lifestyle pattern that will be compatible to that of his human pack (*you!*). Just as we guide little children to learn our way of life, we must show the puppy when it is time to play, eat, sleep, exercise and even entertain himself.

Your puppy should always sleep in his crate. He should

HOUSE-TRAINING TIP

Most of all, be consistent. Always take your dog to the same location, always use the same command and always have the dog on lead when he is in his relief area, unless a fenced-in yard is available.

By following the Success Method, your puppy will be completely house-broken by the time his muscle and brain development reach maturity. Keep in mind that small breeds usually mature faster than large breeds, but all puppies should be trained by six months of age.

also learn that, during times of household confusion and excessive human activity, such as at breakfast when family members are preparing for the day, he can play by himself in relative safety and comfort in his designated area. Each time you leave the puppy alone, he should understand exactly where he is to stay.

Puppies are chewers. They cannot tell the difference between things like lamp cords, television wires, shoes, table legs, etc. Chewing into a television wire, for example, can be fatal to the puppy, while a shorted wire can start a fire in the house. If the puppy chews on the arm of the chair when he is alone, you will probably discipline him angrily when you get home. Thus, he makes the association that your coming home means he is going to be punished. (He will not remember chewing the chair and is incapable of making the association of the discipline with his naughty deed.) Accustoming the pup to his designated area not only keeps him safe but also avoids his engaging in destructive behaviors when you are not around.

Times of excitement, such as special occasions, family parties, etc., can be fun for the puppy, providing that he can view the activities from the security of his designated area. He is not underfoot and he is not being fed all sorts of tidbits that will probably cause him stomach distress, yet he still feels a part of the fun.

SCHEDULE
A puppy should be taken to his relief area each time he is released from his designated

IGs love attention from their owners and don't mind a bit of "babying" from time to time.

area, after meals, after play sessions and when he first awakens in the morning (at age 12 weeks, this can mean 5 a.m.!). The puppy will indicate that he's ready "to go" by circling or sniffing busily—do not misinterpret these signs.

When your pup comes home, a routine of taking him out every hour is necessary. As the puppy grows, he will be able to wait for longer periods of time.

Keep trips to his relief area short. Stay no more than five or six minutes and then return to

THE SUCCESS METHOD

Success that comes by luck is usually short-lived. Success that comes by well-thought-out proven methods is often more easily achieved and permanent. This is the Success Method. It is designed to give you, the puppy owner, a simple yet proven way to help your puppy develop clean living habits and a feeling of security in his new environment.

6 Steps to Successful Crate Training

1 Tell the puppy "Crate time!" and place him in the crate with a small treat (a piece of cheese or half of a biscuit). Let him stay in the crate for five minutes while you are in the same room. Then release him and praise lavishly. Never release him when he is fussing. Wait until he is quiet before you let him out.

2 Repeat Step 1 several times a day.

3 The next day, place the puppy in the crate as before. Let him stay there for ten minutes. Do this several times.

4 Continue building time in five-minute increments until the puppy stays in his crate for 30 minutes with you in the room. Always take him to his relief area after prolonged periods in his crate.

5 Now go back to Step 1 and let the puppy stay in his crate for five minutes, this time while you are out of the room.

6 Once again, build crate time in five-minute increments with you out of the room. When the puppy will stay willingly in his crate (he may even fall asleep!) for 30 minutes with you out of the room, he will be ready to stay in it for several hours at a time.

the house. If he goes during that time, praise him lavishly and take him indoors immediately. If he does not, but he has an accident when you go back indoors, pick him up immediately, say "No! No!" and return to his relief area. Wait a few minutes, then return to the house again. Never hit a puppy or put his face in urine or excrement when he has had an accident!

Once indoors, put the puppy in his crate until you have had time to clean up his accident. Then, release him to the family area and watch him more closely than before. Chances are, his accident was a result of your not picking up his signal or waiting too long before offering him the opportunity to relieve himself. Never hold a grudge against the puppy for accidents.

Let the puppy learn that going outdoors means it is time to relieve himself, not to play. Once trained, he will be able to play indoors and out and still differentiate between the times for play versus the times for relief.

Help him develop regular hours for naps, being alone, playing by himself and just resting, all in his crate. Encourage him to entertain himself while you are busy with your activities. Let him learn that having you near is comforting, but it is not your main purpose in life to provide him with undivided attention.

Each time you put your puppy in his own area, use the same command, whatever suits best. Soon he will run to his crate or special area when he hears you say those words.

Crate training provides safety for you, the puppy and the home. It also provides the puppy with a feeling of security, and that helps the puppy achieve self-confidence and clean habits. Remember that one of the primary ingredients in house-training your puppy is control. Regardless of your lifestyle, there will always be occasions when you will need to have a place where your dog can stay and be happy and safe.

You should train your Italian Greyhound to relieve himself in the same general area of your yard. If you want to be successful, adhere to a daily routine with your dog and he will learn where to "go" in no time.

Crate training is the answer for now and in the future.

In conclusion, a few key elements are really all you need for a successful house-training method—consistency, frequency, praise, control and supervision. By following these procedures

with a normal, healthy puppy, you and the puppy will soon be past the stage of "accidents" and ready to move on to a clean and rewarding life together.

HOW MANY TIMES A DAY?

AGE	RELIEF TRIPS
To 14 weeks	10
14–22 weeks	8
22–32 weeks	6
Adulthood	4
(dog stops growing)	

These are estimates, of course, but they are a guide to the *minimum* number of opportunities a dog should have each day to relieve himself.

ROLES OF DISCIPLINE, REWARD AND PUNISHMENT

Discipline, training one to act in accordance with rules, brings order to life. It is as simple as that. Without discipline, particularly in a group society, chaos will reign supreme and the group will eventually perish. Humans and canines are social animals and need some form of discipline in order to function effectively. They must procure food, protect their home base and reproduce to keep their species going. If there were no discipline in the lives of social animals, they would eventually die from starvation and/or predation by other stronger animals. In the case of domestic canines, discipline in their lives is needed in order for them to understand how their pack (you and other family members) functions and how they must act in order to survive.

A large humane society in a highly populated area recently surveyed dog owners regarding their satisfaction with their relationships with their dogs. People who had trained their dogs were 75% more satisfied with their pets than those who

Provide your IG with safe chew toys to keep him from exercising his jawbones on your valuable possessions or dangerous items.

had never trained their dogs.

Dr. Edward Thorndike, a noted psychologist, established *Thorndike's Theory of Learning*, which states that a behavior that results in a pleasant event tends to be repeated. Likewise, a behavior that results in an unpleasant event tends not to be repeated. It is this theory upon which training methods are based today. For example, if you manipulate a dog to perform a specific behavior and reward him for doing it, he is likely to do it again because he enjoyed the end result.

Occasionally, punishment, a penalty inflicted for an offense, is necessary. The best type of punishment often comes from an outside source. For example, a child is told not to touch the stove because he may get burned. He disobeys and touches the stove. In doing so, he receives a burn. From that time on, he respects the heat of the stove and avoids contact with it. Therefore, a behavior that results in an unpleasant event tends not to be repeated.

A good example of a dog learning the hard way is the dog who chases the house cat. He is told many times to leave the cat alone, yet he persists in teasing the cat. Then, one day, the dog begins chasing the cat but the cat turns and swipes a claw across the dog's face, leaving the dog with a painful gash on his nose. The final result is that the dog stops chasing the cat.

TRAINING EQUIPMENT

COLLAR AND LEAD
For an Italian Greyhound, the collar and lead that you use for training must be one with which you are easily able to work, not too heavy for the dog and perfectly safe.

TREATS
Have a bag of treats on hand; something nutritious and easy

FAMILY TIES
If you have other pets in the home and/or interact often with the pets of friends and other family members, your pup will respond to those pets in much the same manner as you do. It is only when you show fear of or resentment toward another animal that he will act fearful or unfriendly.

to swallow works best. Use a soft treat, a chunk of cheese or a piece of cooked chicken rather than a dry biscuit. By the time the dog has finished chewing a dry treat, he will forget why he is being rewarded in the first place!

It should be noted here that using food rewards will not teach a dog to beg at the table—the only way to teach a dog to beg at the table is to give him food from the table. In training, rewarding the dog with a food treat will help him associate praise and the treats with learning new behaviors that obviously please his owner.

TRAINING BEGINS: ASK THE DOG A QUESTION

In order to teach your dog anything, you must first get his

Practice heeling with your IG, whether he is a companion dog or a show dog. Every dog must learn to walk calmly on the leash.

attention. After all, he cannot learn anything if he is looking away from you with his mind on something else.

To get your dog's attention, ask him "School?" and immediately walk over to him and give him a treat as you tell him "Good dog." Wait a minute or two and repeat the routine, this time with a treat in your hand as you approach within a foot of the dog. Do not go directly to him, but stop about a foot short of him and hold out the treat as you ask "School?" He will see you approaching with a treat in your hand and most likely begin walking toward you. As you meet, give him the treat and praise again.

The third time, ask the question, have a treat in your hand and walk only a short distance toward the dog so that he must walk almost all the way to you. As he reaches you, give him the treat and praise again.

By this time, the dog will probably be getting the idea that if he pays attention to you, especially when you ask that question, it will pay off in treats and enjoyable activities for him. In other words, he learns that "school" means doing great

Your IG's eyes won't leave you as long as you're holding a treat! Food is a surefire attention-getter when teaching a new exercise.

KEEP SMILING

Never train your dog, puppy or adult, when you are angry or in a sour mood. Dogs are very sensitive to human feelings, especially anger, and if your dog senses that you are angry or upset, he will connect your anger with his training and learn to resent or fear his training sessions.

things with you that are fun and that result in positive attention for him.

Remember that the dog does not understand your verbal language; he only recognizes sounds. Your question translates to a series of sounds for him, and those sounds become the signal to go to you and pay attention. The dog learns that if he does this, he will get to interact with you plus receive treats and praise.

THE BASIC COMMANDS

TEACHING SIT
Now that you have the dog's attention, attach his lead and hold it in your left hand, and hold a food treat in your right hand. Place your food hand at the dog's nose and let him lick the treat but not take it from you. Say "Sit" and slowly raise your food hand from in front of

the dog's nose up over his head so that he is looking at the ceiling. As he bends his head upward, he will have to bend his knees to maintain his balance. As he bends his knees, he will assume a sit position. At that point, release the food treat and praise lavishly with comments such as "Good dog! Good sit!" Remember to always praise enthusiastically, because dogs relish verbal praise from their owners and feel so proud of themselves whenever they accomplish a behavior.

Incidentally, you will not use food forever in getting the dog to obey your commands. Food is only used to teach new behaviors and, once the dog knows what you want when you give a specific command, you will wean him off the food treats but still maintain the verbal praise. After all, you will always have your voice with you, and there will be many times when you have no food rewards but expect the dog to obey.

TEACHING DOWN
Teaching the down exercise is easy when you understand how the dog perceives the down position, and it is very difficult when you do not. Dogs perceive the down position as a submissive one; therefore, teaching the down exercise by using a force-

OPEN MINDS
Dogs are as different from each other as people are. What works for one dog may not work for another. Have an open mind. If one method of training is unsuccessful, try another.

ful method can sometimes make the dog develop such a fear of the down that he either runs away when you say "Down" or he attempts to snap at the person who tries to force him down.

Have the dog sit close alongside your left leg, facing in the same direction as you are. Hold the lead in your left hand and a food treat in your right. Now place your left hand lightly on the top of the dog's shoulders where they meet above the spinal cord. Do not push down on the dog's shoulders; simply rest your left hand there so you can guide the dog to lie down close to your left leg rather than

The down command is accomplished with gentle encouragement and patience. Never force an IG into the down position.

you let him sit up again. The goal here is to get the dog to settle down and not feel threatened in the down position.

to swing away from your side when he drops.

Now place the food hand at the dog's nose, say "Down" very softly (almost a whisper) and slowly lower the food hand to the dog's front feet. When the food hand reaches the floor, begin moving it forward along the floor in front of the dog. Keep talking softly to the dog, saying things like, "Do you want this treat? You can do this, good dog." Your reassuring tone of voice will help calm the dog as he tries to follow the food hand in order to get the treat.

When the dog's elbows touch the floor, release the food and praise softly. Try to get the dog to maintain that down position for several seconds before

FEAR AGGRESSION

Pups who are subjected to physical abuse during training commonly end up with behavioral problems as adults. One common result of abuse is fear aggression, in which a dog will lash out, bare his teeth, snarl and finally bite someone by whom he feels threatened. For example, your daughter may be playing with the dog one afternoon. As they play hide-and-seek, she backs the dog into a corner and, as she attempts to tease him playfully, he bites her hand. Examine the cause of this behavior. Did your daughter ever hit the dog? Did someone who resembles your daughter hit or scream at the dog?

Fortunately, fear aggression is relatively easy to correct. Have your daughter engage in only positive activities with the dog, such as feeding, petting and walking. She should not give any corrections or negative feedback. If the dog still growls or cowers away from her, allow someone else to accompany them. After approximately one week, the dog should feel that he can rely on her for many positive things, and he will also be prevented from reacting fearfully towards anyone who might resemble her.

TEACHING STAY

It is easy to teach the dog to stay in either a sit or a down position. Again, we use food and praise during the teaching process as we help the dog to understand exactly what it is that we are expecting him to do.

To teach the sit/stay, start with the dog sitting on your left side as before and hold the lead in your left hand. Have a food treat in your right hand and place your food hand at the dog's nose. Say "Stay" and step out on your right foot to stand directly in front of the dog, toe to toe, as he licks and nibbles the treat. Be sure to keep his head facing upward to maintain the sit position. Count to five and then swing around to stand next to the dog again with him on your left. As soon as you get back to the original position, release the food and praise lavishly.

To teach the down/stay, do the down as previously described. As soon as the dog lies down, say "Stay" and step out on your right foot just as you did in the sit/stay. Count to five and then return to stand beside the dog with him on your left side. Release the treat and praise as always.

Within a week or ten days, you can begin to add a bit of distance between you and your dog when you leave him. When you do, use your left hand open with the palm facing the dog as a stay signal, much the same as the hand signal a police officer uses to stop traffic at an intersection. Hold the food treat in

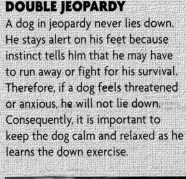

DOUBLE JEOPARDY

A dog in jeopardy never lies down. He stays alert on his feet because instinct tells him that he may have to run away or fight for his survival. Therefore, if a dog feels threatened or anxious, he will not lie down. Consequently, it is important to keep the dog calm and relaxed as he learns the down exercise.

"Pretty please." Is there anything more lovable than an IG who uses his best manners?

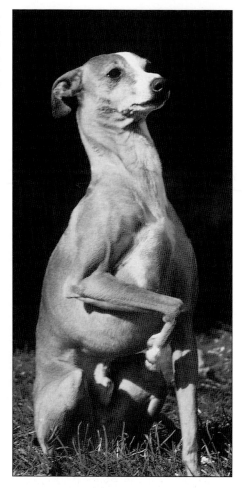

both stays. Eventually, the dog can be expected to remain in the stay position for prolonged periods of time until you return to him or call him to you. Always praise lavishly when he stays.

TEACHING COME

If you make teaching "come" an exciting experience, you should never have a student that does not love the game or that fails to come when called. The secret, it seems, is never to teach the word "come."

At times when an owner most wants his dog to come when called, the owner is likely to be upset or anxious and he allows these feelings to come through in the tone of his voice when he calls his dog. Hearing that desperation in his owner's

your right hand as before, but this time the food will not be touching the dog's nose. He will watch the food hand and quickly learn that he is going to get that treat as soon as you return to his side.

When you can stand 3 feet away from your dog for 30 seconds, you can then begin building time and distance in

CONSISTENCY PAYS OFF

Dogs need consistency in their feeding schedule, exercise and relief visits, and in the verbal commands you use. If you use "Stay" on Monday and "Stay here, please" on Tuesday, you will confuse your dog. Don't demand perfect behavior during training sessions and then let him have the run of the house the rest of the day. Above all, lavish praise on your pet consistently every time he does something right. The more he feels he is pleasing you, the more willing he will be to learn.

"COME" . . . BACK

Never call your dog to come to you for a correction or scold him when he reaches you. That is the quickest way to turn a come command into "Go away fast!" Dogs think only in the present tense, and your dog will connect the scolding with coming to you, not with the misbehavior of a few moments earlier.

locating him. Once the dog learns to love the game, simply calling out "Where are you?" will bring him running from wherever he is when he hears that all-important question.

The come command is recognized as one of the most important things to teach a dog, but there are trainers who work with thousands of dogs and never teach the actual word "come." Yet these dogs will race

voice, the dog fears the results of going to him and therefore either disobeys outright or runs in the opposite direction. The secret, therefore, is to teach the dog a game and, when you want him to come to you, simply play the game. It is practically a no-fail solution!

To begin, have several members of your family take a few food treats and each go into a different room in the house. Everyone takes turns calling the dog, and each person should celebrate the dog's finding him with a treat and lots of happy praise. When a person calls the dog, he is actually inviting the dog to find him and to get a treat as a reward for "winning."

A few turns of the "Where are you?" game and the dog will understand that everyone is playing the game and that each person has a big celebration awaiting the dog's success at

The sit position begins and ends many exercises, which is why it is beneficial to teach this command early in the dog's education.

to respond to a person who uses the dog's name followed by "Where are you?" For example, a woman has a 12-year-old companion dog who went blind, but who never fails to locate her owner when asked, "Where are you?"

Children, in particular, love to play this game with their dogs. Children can hide in smaller places like a shower

Once your IG has been successfully trained to heel on a traditional leash, you can begin to use a flexible one for exercise and regular walks.

> ### THE GOLDEN RULE
> The golden rule of dog training is simple. For each "question" (command), there is only one correct answer (reaction). One command = one reaction. Keep practicing the command until the dog reacts correctly without hesitating. Be repetitive but not monotonous. Dogs get bored just as people do!

stall or bathtub, behind a bed or under a table. The dog needs to work a little bit harder to find these hiding places, but, when he does, he loves to celebrate with a treat and a tussle with a favorite youngster.

TEACHING HEEL

Heeling means that the dog walks beside the owner without pulling. It takes time and patience on the owner's part to succeed at teaching the dog that he (the owner) will not proceed unless the dog is walking calmly beside him. Neither pulling out ahead on the lead nor lagging behind is acceptable.

Begin by holding the lead in your left hand as the dog sits beside your left leg. Move the loop end of the lead to your right hand, but keep your left hand short on the lead so that it keeps the dog in close next to you.

Say "Heel" and step forward on your left foot. Keep the dog close to you and take three steps. Stop and have the dog sit next to you in what we now call the heel position. Praise verbally, but do not touch the dog. Hesitate a moment and begin again with "Heel," taking three steps and stopping, at which point the dog is told to sit again.

Your goal here is to have the dog walk those three steps without pulling on the lead. Once he will walk calmly beside you for three steps without pulling, increase the number of steps you take to five. When he will walk politely beside you while you take five steps, you can increase the length of your walk to ten steps. Keep increasing the length of your stroll until the dog will walk quietly beside you without pulling as long as you want him to heel. When you stop heeling, indicate to the dog that the exercise is over by

Walking two IGs looks easy when they're both heel-trained. When they're not properly trained, it can look like a merry-go-round!

verbally praising as you pet him and say "OK, good dog." The "OK" is used as a release word, meaning that the exercise is finished and the dog is free to relax.

If you are dealing with a dog who insists on pulling you around, simply "put on your brakes" and stand your ground until the dog realizes that the two of you are not going anywhere until he is beside you and moving at your pace, not his. It may take some time just standing there to convince the

TUG OF WALK?

If you begin teaching the heel by taking long walks and letting the dog pull you along, he misinterprets this action as an acceptable form of taking a walk. When you pull back on the leash to counteract his pulling, he reads that tug as a signal to pull even harder!

dog that you are the leader and that you will be the one to decide on the direction and speed of your travel.

Each time the dog looks up at you or slows down to give a slack lead between the two of you, quietly praise him and say, "Good heel. Good dog." Eventually, the dog will begin to respond and within a few days he will be walking politely beside you without pulling on the lead. At first, the training sessions should be kept short and very positive; soon the dog will be able to walk nicely with you for increasingly longer distances. Remember also to give the dog free time and the opportunity to run and play when you have finished heel practice.

WEANING OFF FOOD IN TRAINING

Food is used in training new behaviors. Once the dog understands what behavior goes with a specific command, it is time to start weaning him off the food treats. At first, give a treat after each exercise. Then, start to give a treat only after every other exercise. Mix up the times when you offer a food reward and the times when you only offer praise so that the dog will never know when he is going to receive both food and praise and when he is going to receive only praise. This is called a variable-

HEELING WELL

Teach your dog to heel in an enclosed area, preferably with few distractions, as the naturally curious IG is always ready to investigate. Once you think the dog will obey reliably and you want to attempt advanced obedience exercises such as off-lead heeling, test him in a fenced-in area so he cannot run away.

ratio reward system. It proves successful because there is always the chance that the owner will produce a treat, so the dog never stops trying for that reward. No matter what, *always* give verbal praise.

OBEDIENCE CLASSES

It is a good idea to enroll in an obedience class if one is available in your area. If yours is a show dog, conformation showing classes would be more appropriate. Many areas have dog clubs that offer basic obedience training as well as preparatory classes for obedience competition. There are also local dog trainers who offer similar classes.

At obedience trials, dogs can earn titles at various levels of competition. The beginning levels of obedience competition include basic behaviors such as sit, down, heel, etc. The more advanced levels of competition include jumping, retrieving, scent discrimination and signal work. The advanced levels require a dog and owner to put a lot of time and effort into their training. The titles that can be earned at these levels of competition are very prestigious.

OTHER ACTIVITIES FOR LIFE

Whether a dog is trained in the structured environment of a class or alone with his owner at

HOW TO WEAN THE "TREAT HOG"

If you have trained your dog by rewarding him with a treat each time he performs a command, he may soon decide that without the treat, he won't sit, stay or come. The best way to fix this problem is to start asking your dog to do certain commands twice before being rewarded. Slowly increase the number of commands given and then vary the number: three sits and a treat one day, five sits for a biscuit the next day, etc. Your dog will soon realize that there is no set number of sits before he gets his reward and he'll likely do it the first time you ask In the hope of being rewarded sooner rather than later.

A well-trained IG with a dumbbell, practicing for an obedience event.

home, there are many activities that can bring fun and rewards to both owner and dog once they have mastered basic control.

Teaching the dog to help out around the home, in the yard or on the farm provides great satisfaction to both dog and owner. In addition, the dog's help makes life a little easier for his

FETCH!

Play fetch games with your puppy in an enclosed area where he can retrieve his toy and bring it back to you. Always use a toy or object designated just for this purpose. Never use a shoe, stocking or other item he may later confuse with those in your wardrobe or underneath your chair.

owner and raises his stature as a valued companion to his family. It helps give the dog a purpose by occupying his mind and providing an outlet for his energy.

If you are interested in participating in organized competition with your Italian Greyhound, there are activities other than obedience in which you and your dog can become involved. Agility is a popular sport in which dogs run through an obstacle course that includes various jumps, tunnels and other exercises to test the dog's speed and coordination. When the Italian Greyhound and other small breeds compete in agility, the events are essentially the same as those for larger dogs, except that the obstacles are reduced in size according to the dogs' height. The owners run beside their dogs to give commands and to guide them through the course. Although competitive, the focus is on fun—it's fun to do, fun to watch and great exercise.

Likewise, Italian Greyhounds, as active sighthounds, can participate in various types of coursing and racing events, including lure coursing, which has become increasingly popular with the Whippet set. There are many IGs who have excelled in this fast-paced arena, and it is quite

Many Italian Greyhounds participate in lure-coursing events, which come naturally to sighthounds.

exciting for dog and owner alike. Some training is involved in preparing the IG for the event, though it is not as extensive as agility training. Discuss the possibilities of these events with your breed club, or contact a sighthound club in your area about training and events in which the IG can participate.

With training and ample time, your IG can be taught to participate in sighthound events. These are high-action, exciting events for dogs and spectators alike.

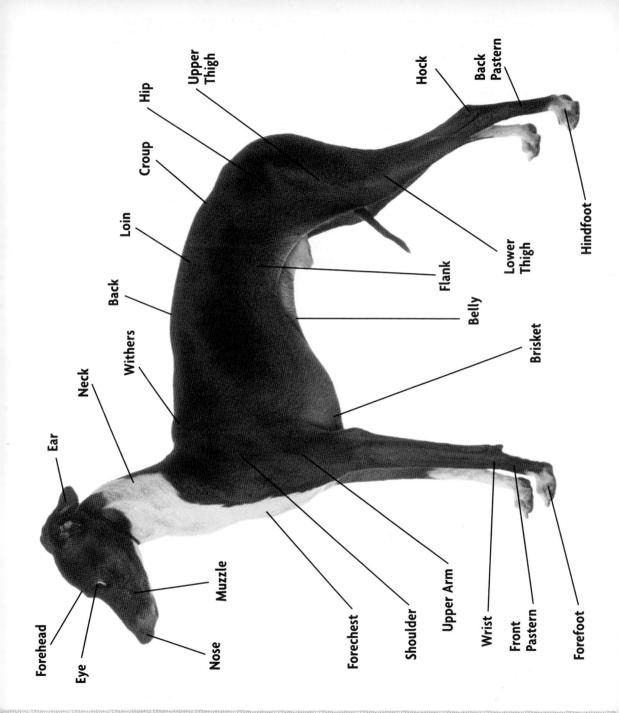

Upper Thigh

Hip

Back Pastern

Hock

Croup

Loin

Hindfoot

Back

Lower Thigh

Flank

Withers

Belly

Neck

Brisket

Ear

Forehead

Eye

Muzzle

Nose

Forechest

Shoulder

Upper Arm

Wrist

Front Pastern

Forefoot

PHYSICAL STRUCTURE OF THE ITALIAN GREYHOUND

Dogs can suffer from many of the same physical illnesses as people. They might even share many of the same psychological problems. Since people usually know more about human diseases than canine maladies, many of the terms used in this chapter will be familiar but not necessarily those used by veterinarians. We will use the term *x-ray*, instead of the more acceptable term *radiograph*. We will also use the familiar term *symptoms* even though dogs don't have symptoms, which are verbal descriptions of the patient's feelings; dogs have *clinical signs*. Since dogs can't speak, we have to look for clinical signs...but we still use the term *symptoms* in this book.

As a general rule, medicine is *practiced*. That term is not arbitrary. Medicine is a constantly changing art as we learn more and more about genetics, electronic aids (like CAT scans and MRIs) and daily laboratory advances. There are many dog maladies, like hip dysplasia, which are not universally treated in the same manner. For example, some vets opt for surgical treatments more often than others.

SELECTING A QUALIFIED VET
Your selection of a veterinarian should be based not only upon his personality but also upon his ability with small dogs and his convenience to your home. You want a vet who is close because you might have emergencies or need to make multiple visits for treatments. You want a vet who has services that you might require such as tattooing and boarding, and of course a good reputation for ability and responsiveness. There is nothing more frustrating than having to wait a day or more to get a response from your vet.

All veterinarians are licensed and their diplomas and/or certificates should be displayed in their waiting rooms. Your vet will deal with all aspects of your dog's health maintenance, injuries, infections, illnesses and the like. Most vets do routine surgery such as neutering, stitching up wounds and docking tails for those breeds in which such is required for show purposes. There are, however, many veterinary specialties that require further studies and internships. These include specialties in heart problems

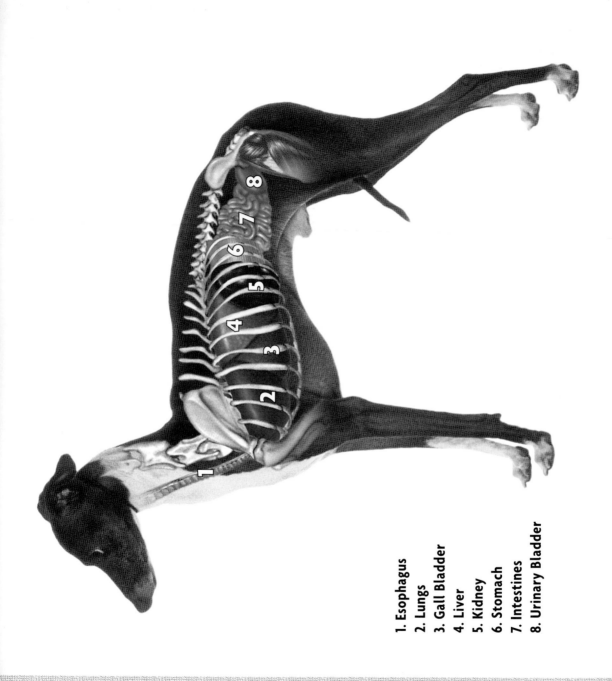

1. Esophagus
2. Lungs
3. Gall Bladder
4. Liver
5. Kidney
6. Stomach
7. Intestines
8. Urinary Bladder

INTERNAL ORGANS OF THE ITALIAN GREYHOUND

(veterinary cardiologists), skin problems (veterinary dermatologists), tooth and gum problems (veterinary dentists), eye problems (veterinary ophthalmologists) and x-rays (veterinary radiologists), as well as vets who have specialties in bones, muscles or certain organs.

When the problem affecting your dog is serious, it is not unusual or impudent to get another medical opinion, although it is courteous to advise the vets concerned about this. You might also want to compare costs among several veterinarians. Sophisticated health care and veterinary services can be very costly. It is not infrequent that important decisions are based upon financial considerations.

PREVENTATIVE MEDICINE
It is much easier, less costly and more effective to practice preventative medicine than to fight bouts of illness and disease. Properly bred puppies come from parents who were selected based upon their genetic-disease profiles. Their mothers should have been vaccinated, free of all internal and external parasites and properly nourished. The dam can pass on disease resistance to her puppies, which can last for eight to ten weeks, but she can also pass on parasites and many infections. Learn as much about the dam's health as you possibly can.

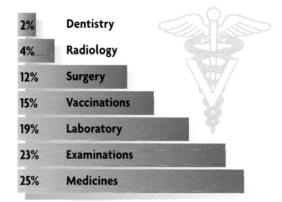

Breakdown of Veterinary Income by Category

2%	Dentistry
4%	Radiology
12%	Surgery
15%	Vaccinations
19%	Laboratory
23%	Examinations
25%	Medicines

WEANING TO BRINGING PUP HOME
Puppies should be weaned by the time they are about two months old. A puppy that remains for at least eight weeks with his dam and littermates usually adapts better to other dogs and people later in life. Some new owners have their puppies examined by veterinarians immediately, either before bringing them home or within the first day or two, which is a good idea.

The puppy will have his teeth examined and have his skeletal conformation and general health checked prior to certification by the vet. Puppies in certain breeds may have problems with their kneecaps, cataracts and other eye problems, heart murmurs or undescended testicles. Your vet might also have training in temperament evaluation. At the first visit, the

A typical vet's income, categorized according to services performed. This survey dealt with small-animal (pets) practices.

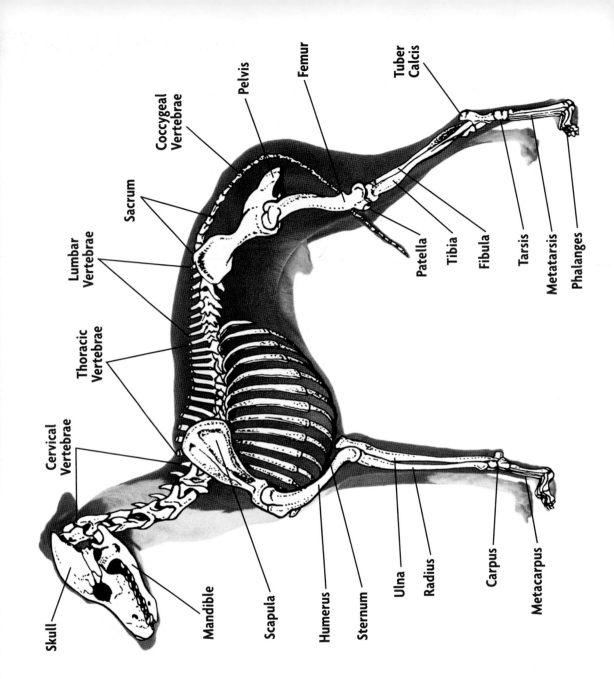

Skull

Cervical Vertebrae

Mandible

Scapula

Humerus

Sternum

Ulna

Radius

Carpus

Metacarpus

Thoracic Vertebrae

Lumbar Vertebrae

Sacrum

Coccygeal Vertebrae

Pelvis

Femur

Tuber Calcis

Patella

Tibia

Fibula

Tarsis

Metatarsis

Phalanges

SKELETAL STRUCTURE OF THE ITALIAN GREYHOUND

vet will set up your pup's vaccination schedule.

VACCINATION SCHEDULING

Most vaccinations are given by injection and should only be done by a veterinarian. Both he and you should keep records of the date of the injection, the identification of the vaccine and the amount given. Some vets give a first vaccination at six weeks, but most dog breeders prefer the course not to commence until about eight weeks to avoid negating any antibodies passed on by the dam. The vaccination scheduling is usually based on a two- to four-week cycle. You must take your vet's advice regarding when to vaccinate, as this may differ according to the vaccine used.

Most vaccinations immunize your puppy against viruses. The usual vaccines contain immunizing doses of several different viruses such as distemper, parvovirus, parainfluenza and hepatitis, although some veterinarians recommend separate vaccines for each disease. There are other vaccines available when the puppy is at risk. You should rely upon professional advice. This is especially true for the booster-shot program. Most vaccination programs require a booster when the puppy is a year old and once a year thereafter. In some cases, circumstances may require more or less frequent immunizations.

Canine cough, more formally known as tracheobronchitis, is treated with a vaccine that is sprayed into the dog's nostrils. Canine cough is usually included in routine vaccinations, but this is often not as effective as the vaccines for other major diseases.

FIVE TO TWELVE MONTHS OF AGE

Unless you intend to breed or show your dog, neutering the puppy around six months of age is recommended. Discuss this with your veterinarian. Neutering and spaying have proven to be extremely beneficial to both male and female dogs. Besides eliminating the possibility of pregnancy and pyometra in bitches and testicular cancer in male dogs, it greatly reduces the risk of breast cancer in bitches and prostate cancer in males.

Your veterinarian should provide your puppy with a thorough dental evaluation at six months of age, ascertaining

VACCINE ALLERGIES

Vaccines do not work all the time. Sometimes dogs are allergic to them and many times the antibodies, which are supposed to be stimulated by the vaccine, just are not produced. You should keep your dog in the veterinary clinic for an hour after he is vaccinated to be sure there are no allergic reactions.

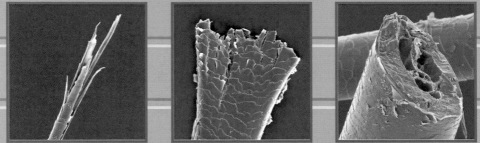

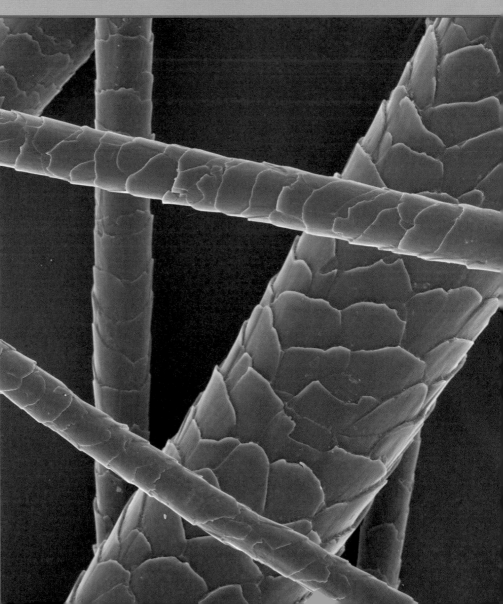

Normal hairs of a dog, enlarged 200 times original size. The cuticle (outer covering) is clean and healthy. Unlike human hair that grows from the base, a dog's hair also grows from the end. Damaged hairs and split ends, illustrated above.

SCANNING ELECTRON MICROGRAPHS BY DR. DENNIS KUNKEL, UNIVERSITY OF HAWAII

whether all of the permanent teeth have erupted properly. A home dental-care regimen should be initiated at six months, including brushing weekly and providing good dental devices (such as nylon bones). Regular dental care promotes healthy teeth, fresh breath and a longer life.

OLDER THAN ONE YEAR

Once a year, your grown dog should visit the vet for an examination and vaccination boosters, if needed. Some vets recommend blood tests, a thyroid level check and a dental evaluation (perhaps including a thorough veterinary tooth-cleaning) to accompany these annual visits. A thorough clinical evaluation by the vet can provide critical background information for your dog. In the long run, quality preventative care for your pet can save money, teeth and lives.

SKIN PROBLEMS

Veterinarians are consulted by dog owners for skin problems more than for any other group of diseases or maladies. Dogs' skin is almost as sensitive as human skin, and both can suffer from almost the same ailments (though the occurrence of acne in most dogs is

HEALTH AND VACCINATION SCHEDULE

AGE IN WEEKS:	6TH	8TH	10TH	12TH	14TH	16TH	20-24TH	52ND
Worm Control	✔	✔	✔	✔	✔	✔	✔	
Neutering							✔	
Heartworm		✔		✔		✔	✔	
Parvovirus	✔		✔		✔		✔	✔
Distemper		✔		✔		✔		✔
Hepatitis		✔		✔		✔		✔
Leptospirosis								✔
Parainfluenza	✔		✔		✔			✔
Dental Examination		✔					✔	✔
Complete Physical		✔					✔	✔
Coronavirus				✔			✔	✔
Canine Cough	✔							
Hip Dysplasia							✔	
Rabies							✔	

Vaccinations are not instantly effective. It takes about two weeks for the dog's immune system to develop antibodies. Most vaccinations require annual booster shots. Your vet should guide you in this regard.

rare). For this reason, veterinary dermatology has developed into a specialty practiced by many vets.

Since many skin problems have visual symptoms that are almost identical, it requires the skill of an experienced veterinary dermatologist to identify and cure many of the more severe skin disorders. Pet shops sell many treatments for skin problems, but most of the treatments are directed at the symptoms and not the underlying problem(s). If your dog is suffering from a skin disorder, you should seek professional assistance as quickly as possible. As with all diseases, the earlier a problem is identified and treated, the more likely it is that the cure will be successful.

HEREDITARY SKIN DISORDERS

Veterinary dermatologists are currently researching a number of skin disorders that are believed to have a hereditary basis. These inherited diseases are transmitted by both parents, who appear (phenotypically) normal but have a recessive gene for the disease, meaning that they carry, but are not affected by, the disease. These diseases pose serious problems to breeders because in some instances there are no methods of identifying carriers. Often the secondary diseases associated with these skin conditions are even more debilitating than the skin disorders themselves,

including cancers and respiratory problems.

Color dilution alopecia, the most concerning hereditary disorder, affects blue Italian Greyhounds and other similarly colored dogs. Among the other hereditary skin disorders, for which the mode of inheritance is known, are acrodermatitis, cutaneous asthenia (Ehlers-Danlos syndrome), sebaceous adenitis, cyclic hematopoiesis, dermatomyositis, IgA deficiency and nodular dermatofibrosis. Some of these disorders are limited to one or two breeds, while others affect a large number of breeds. All inherited diseases must be diagnosed and treated by a veterinary specialist.

PARASITE BITES

Many of us are allergic to insect bites. The bites itch, erupt and may even become infected. Dogs have the same reaction to fleas, ticks and/or mites. When an insect lands on you, you have the chance to whisk it away with your hand. Unfortunately, when your dog is bitten by a flea, tick or mite, he can only scratch it away or bite it. By the time the dog has been bitten, the parasite has done some of its damage. It may also have laid eggs, which will cause further problems in the near future. The itching from parasite bites is probably due to the saliva injected into the site

DISEASE REFERENCE CHART

	What is it?	What causes it?	Symptoms
Leptospirosis	Severe disease that affects the internal organs; can be spread to people.	A bacterium, which is often carried by rodents, that enters through mucous membranes and spreads quickly throughout the body.	Range from fever, vomiting and loss of appetite in less severe cases to shock, irreversible kidney damage and possibly death in most severe cases.
Rabies	Potentially deadly virus that infects warm-blooded mammals.	Bite from a carrier of the virus, mainly wild animals.	1st stage: dog exhibits change in behavior, fear. 2nd stage: dog's behavior becomes more aggressive. 3rd stage: loss of coordination, trouble with bodily functions.
Parvovirus	Highly contagious virus, potentially deadly.	Ingestion of the virus, which is usually spread through the feces of infected dogs.	Most common: severe diarrhea. Also vomiting, fatigue, lack of appetite.
Canine cough	Contagious respiratory infection.	Combination of types of bacteria and virus. Most common: *Bordetella bronchiseptica* bacteria and parainfluenza virus.	Chronic cough.
Distemper	Disease primarily affecting respiratory and nervous system.	Virus that is related to the human measles virus.	Mild symptoms such as fever, lack of appetite and mucus secretion progress to evidence of brain damage, "hard pad."
Hepatitis	Virus primarily affecting the liver.	Canine adenovirus type I (CAV-1). Enters system when dog breathes in particles.	Lesser symptoms include listlessness, diarrhea, vomiting. More severe symptoms include "blue-eye" (clumps of virus in eye).
Coronavirus	Virus resulting in digestive problems.	Virus is spread through infected dog's feces.	Stomach upset evidenced by lack of appetite, vomiting, diarrhea.

when the parasite sucks the dog's blood.

AUTO-IMMUNE SKIN CONDITIONS

An auto-immune skin condition is commonly referred to as a condition in which a person (or dog) is allergic to himself, while an allergy is usually an inflammatory reaction to an outside stimulus. Auto-immune diseases cause serious damage to the tissues that are involved.

The best known auto-immune disease is lupus, which affects people as well as dogs. The symptoms are variable and may affect the kidneys, bones, blood chemistry and skin. It can be fatal to both dogs and humans, though it is not thought to be transmissible. It is usually successfully treated with cortisone, prednisone or a similar corticosteroid, but extensive use of these drugs can have harmful side effects.

AIRBORNE ALLERGIES

Just as humans have hay fever, rose fever and other fevers from

PET ADVANTAGES

If you do not intend to show or breed your new puppy, your veterinarian will probably recommend that you spay your female or neuter your male. Some people believe neutering leads to weight gain, but if you feed and exercise your dog properly, this is easily avoided. Spaying or neutering can actually have many positive outcomes, such as:

- training becomes easier, as the dog focuses less on the urge to mate and more on you!
- females are protected from unplanned pregnancy as well as ovarian and uterine cancers.
- males are guarded from testicular tumors and have a reduced risk of developing prostate cancer.

Talk to your vet regarding the right age to spay/neuter and other aspects of the procedure.

which they suffer during the pollinating season, many dogs suffer from the same allergies. When the pollen count is high, your dog might suffer, but don't expect him to sneeze and have a runny nose like a human would. Dogs react to pollen allergies the same way they react to fleas—they scratch and bite themselves.

Dogs, like humans, can be tested for allergens. Discuss the testing with your veterinary dermatologist.

FOOD PROBLEMS

FOOD ALLERGIES

Dogs can be allergic to many foods that are best-sellers and highly recommended by breeders and veterinarians. Changing the brand of food that you buy may not eliminate the problem if the element to which the dog is allergic is contained in the new brand.

Recognizing a food allergy is difficult. Humans vomit or have rashes when they eat a food to which they are allergic. Dogs neither vomit nor (usually) develop rashes. They react in the same manner as they would to an airborne or flea allergy; they itch, scratch and bite, thus making the diagnosis extremely difficult. While pollen allergies and parasite bites are usually seasonal, food allergies are year-round problems.

FOOD INTOLERANCE

Food intolerance is the inability of the dog to completely digest certain foods. Puppies that may have done very well on their mother's milk may not do well on cow's milk. The results of food intolerance may be evident in loose bowels, passing gas and stomach pains. These are the only obvious symptoms of food intolerance, which makes diagnosis difficult.

TREATING FOOD PROBLEMS

It is possible to handle food allergies and food intolerance yourself.

Start by putting your dog on a diet that he has never had. Obviously, if the dog has never eaten this new food, he can't yet have been allergic or intolerant of it. Start with a single ingredient that is not in the dog's diet at the present time. Ingredients like chopped beef or chicken are common in dogs' diets, so try a different protein source like lamb or fish. Keep the dog on this diet (with no additives) for a month. If the symptoms of food allergy or intolerance disappear, it is quite likely that your dog has a food allergy.

Don't think that the single ingredient cured the problem. You still must find a suitable diet and ascertain which ingredient in the old diet was objectionable. This is most easily done by adding ingredients to the new diet one at a time. Let the dog stay on the modified diet for a month before you add another ingredient. Eventually, you will determine the ingredient that caused the adverse reaction.

An alternative method is to carefully study the ingredients in the diet to which your dog is allergic or intolerant. Identify the main ingredient in this diet and eliminate the main ingredient by buying a different food that does not have that ingredient. Keep experimenting until the symptoms disappear after one month on the new diet.

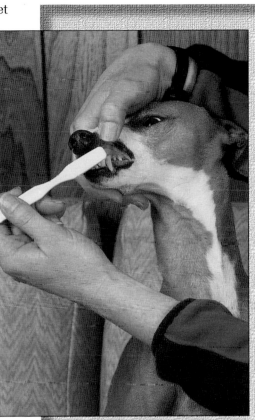

CARETAKER OF TEETH

You are your dog's caretaker and his dentist. Vets warn that plaque and tartar buildup on the teeth will damage the gums and allow bacteria to enter the dog's bloodstream, causing serious damage to the animal's vital organs. Studies show that over 50 percent of dogs have some form of gum disease before age three. Daily or weekly tooth cleaning (with a brush or soft gauze pad wipes) can add to your dog's life.

A male dog flea, *Ctenocephalides canis.*

PHOTO BY JEAN CLAUDE REVY/PHOTOTAKE.

EXTERNAL PARASITES

FLEAS

Of all the problems to which dogs are prone, none is more well known and frustrating than fleas. Flea infestation is relatively simple to cure but difficult to prevent. Parasites that are harbored inside the body are a bit more difficult to eradicate but they are easier to control.

To control flea infestation, you have to understand the flea's life cycle. Fleas are often thought of as a summertime problem, but centrally heated homes have changed the patterns and fleas can be found at any time of the year. The most effective method of flea control is a two-stage approach: one stage to kill the adult fleas, and the other to control the development of pre-adult fleas. Unfortunately, no single active ingredient is effective against all stages of the life cycle.

FLEA KILLER CAUTION— "POISON"

Flea-killers are poisonous. You should not spray these toxic chemicals on areas of a dog's body that he licks, including his genitals and his face. Flea killers taken internally are a better answer, but check with your vet in case internal therapy is not advised for your dog.

LIFE CYCLE STAGES

During its life, a flea will pass through four life stages: egg, larva, pupa or nymph and adult. The adult stage is the most visible and irritating stage of the flea life cycle, and this is why the majority of flea-control products concentrate on this stage. The fact is that adult fleas account for only 1% of the total flea population, and the other 99% exist in pre-adult stages, i.e., eggs, larvae and nymphs. The pre-adult stages are barely visible to the naked eye.

THE LIFE CYCLE OF THE FLEA

Eggs are laid on the dog, usually in quantities of about 20 or 30, several times a day. The adult female flea must have a blood meal before each egg-laying session. When first laid, the eggs will cling to the dog's hair, as the eggs are still moist. However, they will quickly dry out and fall from the dog, especially if the dog moves around or scratches. Many eggs will fall off in the dog's favorite area or an area in which he spends a lot of time, such as his bed.

Once the eggs fall from the dog onto the carpet or furniture, they will hatch into larvae. This takes from one to ten days. Larvae are not particularly mobile and will usually travel only a few inches from where they hatch. However, they do have a tendency to move away from bright light and heavy

EN GARDE: CATCHING FLEAS OFF GUARD!
Consider the following ways to arm yourself against fleas:
- Add a small amount of pennyroyal or eucalyptus oil to your dog's bath. These natural remedies repel fleas.
- Supplement your dog's food with fresh garlic (minced or grated) and a hearty amount of brewer's yeast, both of which ward off fleas.
- Use a flea comb on your dog daily. Submerge fleas in a cup of bleach to kill them quickly.
- Confine the dog to only a few rooms to limit the spread of fleas in the home.
- Vacuum daily...and get all of the crevices! Dispose of the bag every few days until the problem is under control.
- Wash your dog's bedding daily. Cover cushions where your dog sleeps with towels, and wash the towels often.

traffic—under furniture and behind doors are common places to find high quantities of flea larvae.

The flea larvae feed on dead organic matter, including adult flea feces, until they are ready to change into adult fleas. Fleas will usually remain as larvae for around seven days. After this period, the larvae will pupate into protective pupae. While inside the pupae, the larvae will undergo metamorphosis and change into adult fleas. This can take as little time as a few days, but the adult fleas can remain inside the pupae waiting to hatch for up to two years. The pupae are signaled to hatch by certain stimuli, such as physical pressure—the pupae's being stepped on, heat from an animal's lying on the pupae or increased carbon-dioxide levels and vibrations—indicating that a suitable host is available.

Once hatched, the adult flea must feed within a few days. Once the adult flea finds a host, it will not leave voluntarily. It only becomes dislodged by grooming or the host animal's scratching. The adult flea will remain on the

PHOTO BY DWIGHT R. KUHN

host for the duration of its life unless forcibly removed.

TREATING THE ENVIRONMENT AND THE DOG

Treating fleas should be a two-pronged attack. First, the environment needs to be treated; this includes carpets and furniture, especially the dog's bedding and areas underneath furniture. The environment should be treated with a household spray containing an Insect Growth Regulator (IGR) and an insecticide to kill the adult fleas. Most IGRs are effective against eggs and larvae; they actually mimic the fleas' own hormones and stop the eggs and larvae from developing into adult fleas. There are currently no treatments available to attack the pupa stage of the life cycle, so the adult insecticide is used to kill the newly hatched adult fleas before they find a host. Most IGRs are active for many months, while adult insecticides are only active

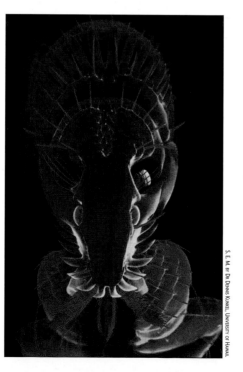

A scanning electron micrograph of a dog or cat flea, *Ctenocephalides*, magnified more than 100x. This image has been colorized for effect.

S. E. M. BY DR. DENNIS KUNKEL, UNIVERSITY OF HAWAII

THE LIFE CYCLE OF THE FLEA

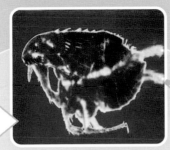

Adult

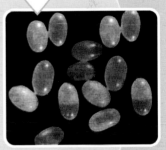

Egg

Larva

Pupa or Nymph

Fleas have been around for millions of years and have adapted to changing host animals. They are able to go through a complete life cycle in less than one month or they can extend their lives to almost two years by remaining as pupae or cocoons. They do not need blood or any other food for up to 20 months.

INSECT GROWTH REGULATOR (IGR)

Two types of products should be used when treating fleas—a product to treat the pet and a product to treat the home. Adult fleas represent less than 1% of the flea population. The pre-adult fleas (eggs, larvae and pupae) represent more than 99% of the flea population and are found in the environment; it is in the case of pre-adult fleas that products containing an Insect Growth Regulator (IGR) should be used in the home.

IGRs are a new class of compounds used to prevent the development of insects. They do not kill the insect outright, but instead use the insect's biology against it to stop it from completing its growth. Products that contain methoprene are the world's first and leading IGRs. Used to control fleas and other insects, this type of IGR will stop flea larvae from developing and protect the house for up to seven months.

The American dog tick, *Dermacentor variabilis*, is probably the most common tick found on dogs. Look at the strength in its eight legs! No wonder it's hard to detach them.

is to apply an adult insecticide to the dog. Traditionally, this would be in the form of a collar or a spray, but more recent innovations include digestible insecticides that poison the fleas when they ingest the dog's blood. Alternatively, there are drops that, when placed on the back of the dog's neck, spread throughout the hair and skin to kill adult fleas.

TICKS

Though not as common as fleas, ticks are found all over the tropical and temperate world. They don't bite, like fleas; they harpoon. They dig their sharp proboscis (nose) into the dog's skin and drink the blood. Their only food and drink is dog's

for a few days.

When treating with a household spray, it is a good idea to vacuum before applying the product. This stimulates as many pupae as possible to hatch into adult fleas. The vacuum cleaner should also be treated with an insecticide to prevent the eggs and larvae that have been collected in the vacuum bag from hatching.

The second stage of treatment

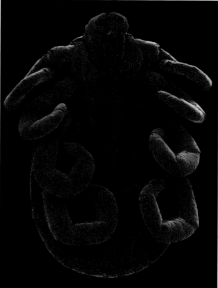

S. E. M. by Dr. Dennis Kunkel, University of Hawaii.

blood. Dogs can get Lyme disease, Rocky Mountain spotted fever, tick bite paralysis and many other diseases from ticks. They may live where fleas are found and they like to hide in cracks or seams in walls. They are controlled the same way fleas are controlled.

The American dog tick, *Dermacentor variabilis*, may well be the most common dog tick in many geographical areas, especially those areas where the climate is hot and humid. Most dog ticks have life expectancies of a week to six months, depending upon climatic conditions. They can neither jump nor fly, but they can crawl slowly and can range up to 16 feet to reach a sleeping or unsuspecting dog.

MITES

Just as fleas and ticks can be problematic for your dog, mites can also lead to an itchy nuisance. Microscopic in size, mites are related to ticks and generally take up permanent residence on their host animal—in this case, your dog! The term *mange* refers to any infestation caused by one of the mighty mites, of which there are six varieties that concern dog owners.

Demodex mites cause a condition known as demodicosis (sometimes called red mange or

DEER-TICK CROSSING
The great outdoors may be fun for your dog, but it also is a home to dangerous ticks. Deer ticks carry a bacterium known as *Borrelia burgdorferi* and are most active in the autumn and spring. When infections are caught early, penicillin and tetracycline are effective antibiotics, but, if left untreated, the bacteria may cause neurological, kidney and cardiac problems as well as long-term trouble with walking and painful joints.

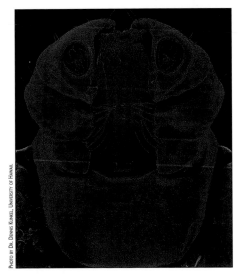

The head of an American dog tick, *Dermacentor variabilis*, enlarged and colorized for effect.

The mange mite, *Psoroptes bovis*, can infest cattle and other domestic animals.

PHOTO BY JAMES HAYDEN/YOAV/PHOTOTAKE.

follicular mange), in which the mites live in the dog's hair follicles and sebaceous glands in larger-than-normal numbers. This type of mange is commonly passed from the dam to her puppies and usually shows up on the puppies' muzzles, though demodicosis is not transferable from one normal dog to another. Most dogs recover from this type of mange without any treatment, though topical therapies are commonly prescribed by the vet.

The *Cheyletiellosis* mite is the hook-mouthed culprit associated with "walking dandruff," a condition that affects dogs as well as cats and rabbits. This mite lives on the surface of the animal's skin and is readily transferable through direct or indirect contact with an affected animal. The dandruff is present in the form of scaly skin, which may or may not be itchy. If not treated, this mange can affect a whole kennel of dogs and can be spread to humans as well.

The *Sarcoptes* mite causes intense itching on the dog in the form of a condition known as scabies or sarcoptic mange. The cycle of the *Sarcoptes* mite lasts about three weeks, and the mites live in the top layer of the dog's skin (epidermis), preferably in

Human lice look like dog lice; the two are closely related.

PHOTO BY DWIGHT R. KUHN.

areas with little hair. Scabies is highly contagious and can be passed to humans. Sometimes an allergic reaction to the mite worsens the severe itching associated with sarcoptic mange.

Ear mites, *Otodectes cynotis,* lead to otodectic mange, which most commonly affects the outer ear canal of the dog, though other areas can be affected as well. Dogs with ear-mite infestation commonly scratch at their ears, causing further irritation, and shake their heads. Dark brown droppings in the outer ear confirm the diagnosis. Your vet can prescribe a treatment to flush out the ears and kill any eggs in the ears. A complete month of treatment is necessary to cure the mange.

Two other mites, less common in dogs, include *Dermanyssus gallinae* (the poultry or red mite) and *Eutrombicula alfreddugesi* (the North American mite associated with trombiculidiasis or chigger infestation). The poultry mite frequently lives on chickens, but can transfer to dogs who spend time near farm animals. Chigger infestation affects dogs in the

NOT A DROP TO DRINK

Never allow your dog to swim in polluted water or public areas where water quality can be suspect. Even perfectly clear water can harbor parasites, many of which can cause serious to fatal illnesses in canines. Areas inhabited by waterfowl and other wildlife are especially dangerous.

central US who have exposure to woodlands. The types of mange caused by both of these mites are treatable by vets.

INTERNAL PARASITES

Most animals—fishes, birds and mammals, including dogs and humans—have worms and other parasites that live inside their bodies. According to Dr. Herbert R. Axelrod, the fish pathologist, there are two kinds of parasites: dumb and smart. The smart parasites live in peaceful cooperation with their hosts (symbiosis), while the dumb parasites kill their hosts. Most worm infections are relatively easy to control. If they are not controlled, they weaken the host dog to the point that other medical problems occur, but they do not kill the host as dumb parasites would.

A brown dog tick, *Rhipicephalus sanguineus*, is an uncommon but annoying tick found on dogs.

Photo by Carolina Biological Supply/Phototake

DO NOT MIX

Never mix parasite-control products without first consulting your vet. Some products can become toxic when combined with others and can cause fatal consequences.

The roundworm *Rhabditis* can infect both dogs and humans.

The roundworm, *Ascaris lumbricoides.*

ROUNDWORMS

Average-size dogs can pass 1,360,000 roundworm eggs every day. For example, if there were only 1 million dogs in the world, the world would be saturated with thousands of tons of dog feces. These feces would contain around 15,000,000,000 roundworm eggs.

Up to 31% of home yards and children's sand boxes in the US contain roundworm eggs.

Flushing dog's feces down the toilet is not a safe practice because the usual sewage treatments do not destroy roundworm eggs.

Infected puppies start shedding roundworm eggs at three weeks of age. They can be infected by their mother's milk.

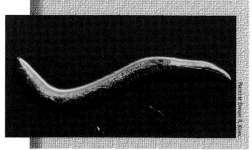

ROUNDWORMS

The roundworms that infect dogs are known scientifically as *Toxocara canis.* They live in the dog's intestines and shed eggs continually. It has been estimated that a dog produces about 6 or more ounces of feces every day. Each ounce of feces averages hundreds of thousands of roundworm eggs. There are no known areas in which dogs roam that do not contain roundworm eggs. The greatest danger of roundworms is that they infect people, too! It is wise to have your dog tested regularly for roundworms.

In young puppies, roundworms cause bloated bellies, diarrhea, coughing and vomiting, and are transmitted from the dam (through blood or milk). Affected puppies will not appear as animated as normal puppies. The worms appear spaghetti-like, measuring as long as 6 inches. Adult dogs can acquire roundworms through coprophagia (eating contaminated feces) or by killing rodents that carry roundworms.

Roundworm infection can kill puppies and cause severe problems in adults, as the hatched larvae travel to the lungs and trachea through the bloodstream. Cleanliness is the best preventative for roundworms. Always pick up after your dog and dispose of feces in appropriate receptacles.

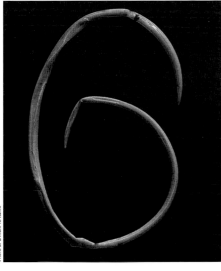

PHOTO BY DWIGHT R. KUHN.

HOOKWORMS

In the United States, dog owners have to be concerned about four different species of hookworm, the most common and most serious of which is *Ancylostoma caninum*, which prefers warm climates. The others are *Ancylostoma braziliense*, *Ancylostoma tubaeforme* and *Uncinaria stenocephala*, the latter of which is a concern to dogs living in the northern US and Canada, as this species prefers cold climates.

Hookworms are dangerous to humans as well as to dogs and cats, and can be the cause of severe anemia due to iron deficiency. The worm uses its teeth to attach itself to the dog's intestines and changes the site of its attachment about six times per day. Each time the worm repositions

itself, the dog loses blood and can become anemic. *Ancylostoma caninum* is the most likely of the four species to cause anemia in the dog.

Symptoms of hookworm infection include dark stools, weight loss, general weakness, pale coloration and anemia, as well as possible skin problems. Fortunately, hookworms are easily purged from the affected dog with a number of medications that have proven effective. Discuss these with your vet. Most heartworm preventatives include a hookworm insecticide as well.

Owners also must be aware that hookworms can infect humans, who can acquire the larvae through exposure to contaminated feces. Since the worms cannot complete their life cycle on a human, the worms simply infest the skin and cause irritation. This condition is known as cutaneous larva migrans syndrome. As a preventative, use disposable gloves or a "poop-scoop" to pick up your dog's droppings and prevent your dog (or neighborhood cats) from defecating in children's play areas.

The hookworm, *Ancylostoma caninum*.

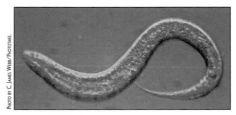

PHOTO BY C. JAMES WEBB/PHOTOTAKE.

The infective stage of the hookworm larva.

TAPEWORMS

Humans, rats, squirrels, foxes, coyotes, wolves and domestic dogs are all susceptible to tapeworm infection. Except in humans, tapeworms are usually not a fatal infection. Infected individuals can harbor 1000 parasitic worms.

Tapeworms, like some other types of worm, are hermaphroditic, meaning male and female in the same worm.

If dogs eat infected rats or mice, or anything else infected with tapeworm, they get the tapeworm disease. One month after attaching to a dog's intestine, the worm starts shedding eggs. These eggs are infective immediately. Infective eggs can live for a few months without a host animal.

The head and rostellum (the round prominence on the scolex) of a tapeworm, which infects dogs and humans.

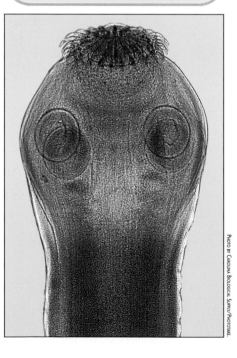

Photo by Carolina Biological Supply/Phototake

TAPEWORMS

There are many species of tapeworm, all of which are carried by fleas! The most common tapeworm affecting dogs is known as *Dipylidium caninum*. The dog eats the flea and starts the tapeworm cycle. Humans can also be infected with tapeworms—so don't eat fleas! Fleas are so small that your dog could pass them onto your hands, your plate or your food and thus make it possible for you to ingest a flea that is carrying tapeworm eggs.

While tapeworm infection is not life-threatening in dogs (smart parasite!), it can be the cause of a very serious liver disease for humans. About 50% of the humans infected with *Echinococcus multilocularis*, a type of tapeworm that causes alveolar hydatid, perish.

WHIPWORMS

In North America, whipworms are counted among the most common parasitic worms in dogs. The whipworm's scientific name is *Trichuris vulpis*. These worms attach themselves in the lower parts of the intestine, where they feed. Affected dogs may only experience upset tummies, colic and diarrhea. These worms, however, can live for months or years in the dog, beginning their larval stage in the small intestine, spending their adult stage in the large intestine and finally passing infective eggs through the dog's feces. The only way to detect whipworms is through a fecal examination, though this is not always foolproof. Treatment for whipworms is tricky, due to the worms' unusual life-cycle pattern, and very often dogs are reinfected due to exposure to infective eggs on the ground. The whipworm eggs can survive in the environment for as long as five years; thus, cleaning up droppings in your own backyard as well as in public places is absolutely essential for sanitation purposes and the health of your dog and others.

THREADWORMS
Though less common than round-worms, hookworms and those previously mentioned, thread-worms concern dog owners in the southwestern US and Gulf Coast area where the climate is hot and humid. Living in the small intestine of the dog, this worm measures a mere 2 millimeters and is round in shape. Like that of the whipworm, the threadworm's life cycle is very complex and the eggs and larvae are passed through the feces. A deadly disease in humans, *Strongyloides* readily infects people, and the handling of feces is the most common means of transmission. Threadworms are most often seen in young puppies; bloody diarrhea and pneumonia are symptoms. Sick puppies must be isolated and treated immediately; vets recommend a follow-up treatment one month later.

HEARTWORM PREVENTATIVES

There are many heartworm preventatives on the market, many of which are sold at your veterinarian's office. These products can be given daily or monthly, depending on the manufacturer's instructions. All of these preventatives contain chemical insecticides directed at killing heartworms, which leads to some controversy among dog owners. In effect, heartworm preventatives are necessary evils, though you should determine how necessary based on your pet's lifestyle. There is no doubt that heartworm is a dreadful disease that threatens the lives of dogs. However, the likelihood of your dog's being bitten by an infected mosquito is slim in most places, and a mosquito-repellent (or an herbal remedy such as Wormwood or Black Walnut) is much safer for your dog and will not compromise his immune system (the way heartworm preventatives will). Should you decide to use the traditional preventative "medications," you can consider giving the pill every other or third month. Since the toxins in the pill will kill the heartworms at all stages of development, the pill would be effective in killing larvae, nymphs or adults, and it takes four months for the larvae to reach the adult stage. Thus, there is no rationale to poisoning the dog's system on a monthly basis. Lastly, do not give the pill during the winter months since there are no mosquitoes around to pass on their infection, unless you live in a tropical environment.

Life Cycle of the Heartworm

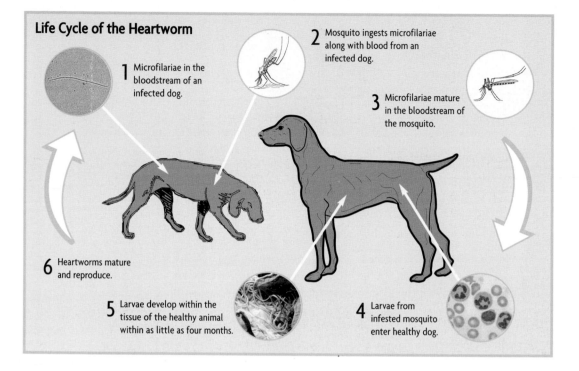

1 Microfilariae in the bloodstream of an infected dog.

2 Mosquito ingests microfilariae along with blood from an infected dog.

3 Microfilariae mature in the bloodstream of the mosquito.

6 Heartworms mature and reproduce.

5 Larvae develop within the tissue of the healthy animal within as little as four months.

4 Larvae from infested mosquito enter healthy dog.

HEARTWORMS

Heartworms are thin, extended worms up to 12 inches long, which live in a dog's heart and the major blood vessels surrounding it. Dogs may have up to 200 worms. Symptoms may be loss of energy, loss of appetite, coughing, the development of a pot belly and anemia.

Heartworms are transmitted by mosquitoes. The mosquito drinks the blood of an infected dog and takes in larvae with the blood. The larvae, called microfilariae, develop within the body of the mosquito and are passed on to the next dog bitten after the larvae mature. It takes two to three weeks for the larvae to develop to the infective stage within the body of the mosquito. Dogs are usually treated at about six weeks of age and maintained on a prophylactic dose given monthly.

Blood testing for heartworms is not necessarily indicative of how seriously your dog is infected. Although this is a dangerous disease, it is not easy for a dog to be infected. Discuss the various preventatives with your vet, as there are many different types now available. Together you can decide on a safe course of prevention for your dog.

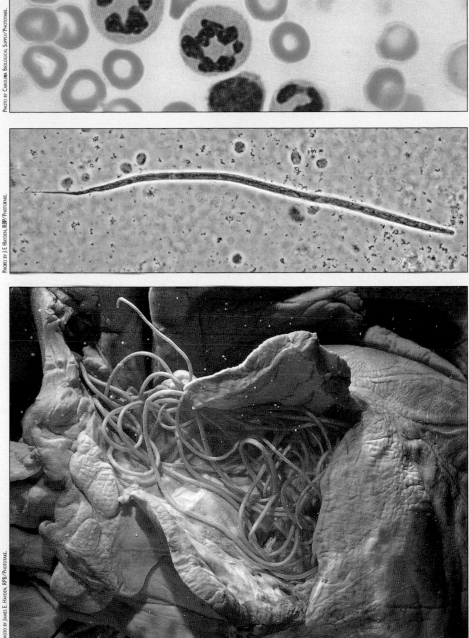

Magnified heartworm larvae, *Dirofilaria immitis.*

Heartworm, *Dirofilaria immitis.*

The heart of a dog infected with canine heartworm, *Dirofilaria immitis.*

HOMEOPATHY:
an alternative to conventional medicine

"Less is Most"

Using this principle, the strength of a homeopathic remedy is measured by the number of serial dilutions that were undertaken to create it. The greater the number of serial dilutions, the greater the strength of the homeopathic remedy. The potency of a remedy that has been made by making a dilution of 1 part in 100 parts (or 1/100) is 1c or 1cH. If this remedy is subjected to a series of further dilutions, each one being 1/100, a more dilute and stronger remedy is produced. If the remedy is diluted in this way six times, it is called 6c or 6cH. A dilution of 6c is 1 part in 1,000,000,000,000. In general, higher potencies in more frequent doses are better for acute symptoms and lower potencies in more infrequent doses are more useful for chronic, long-standing problems.

CURING OUR DOGS NATURALLY

Holistic medicine means treating the whole animal as a unique, perfect, living being. Generally, holistic treatments do not suppress the symptoms that the body naturally produces, as do most medications prescribed by conventional doctors and vets. Holistic methods seek to cure disease by regaining balance and harmony in the patient's environment. Some of these methods include use of nutritional therapy, herbs, flower essences, aromatherapy, acupuncture, massage, chiropractic and, of course, the most popular holistic approach, homeopathy.

Homeopathy is a theory or system of treating illness with small doses of substances which, if administered in larger quantities, would produce the symptoms that the patient already has. This approach is often described as "like cures like." Although modern veterinary medicine is geared toward the "quick fix," homeopathy relies on the belief that, given the time, the body is able to heal itself and return to its natural, healthy state.

Choosing a remedy to cure a problem in our dogs is the difficult part of homeopathy. Consult with your vet for a professional diagnosis of your dog's symptoms. Often these symptoms require immediate conventional care. If your vet is willing and knowledgeable, you may attempt a homeopathic remedy. Be aware that cortisone prevents homeopathic remedies from working. There are hundreds of possibilities and combinations to cure many problems in dogs, from basic physical problems such as excessive shedding, fleas or other parasites, unattractive doggy odor, bad breath, upset tummy, obesity, dry, oily or dull coat, diarrhea, ear problems and eye discharge (including tears and dry or mucousy matter), to behavioral abnormalities such as fear of loud noises, habitual licking, poor appetite, excessive barking and various phobias. From alumina to zincum metallicum, the remedies span the planet and the imagination…from flowers and weeds to chemicals, insect droppings, diesel smoke and volcanic ash.

Using "Like to Treat Like"

Unlike conventional medicines that suppress symptoms, homeopathic remedies treat illnesses with small doses of substances that, if administered in larger quantities, would produce the symptoms that the patient already has. While the same homeopathic remedy can be used to treat different symptoms in different dogs, here are some interesting remedies and their uses.

Apis Mellifica
(made from honey bee venom) can be used for allergies or to reduce swelling that occurs in acutely infected kidneys.

Diesel Smoke
can be used to help control travel sickness.

Calcarea Fluorica
(made from calcium fluoride, which helps harden bone structure) can be useful in treating hard lumps in tissues.

Natrum Muriaticum
(made from common salt, sodium chloride) is useful in treating thin, thirsty dogs.

Nitricum Acidum
(made from nitric acid) is used for symptoms you would expect to see from contact with acids, such as lesions, especially where the skin joins the linings of body orifices or openings such as the lips and nostrils.

Symphytum
(made from the herb Knitbone, *Symphytum officinale*) is used to encourage bones to heal.

Urtica Urens
(made from the common stinging nettle) is used in treating painful, irritating rashes.

First Aid at a Glance

Burns
Place the affected area under cool water; use ice if only a small area is burnt.

Bee stings/Insect bites
Apply ice to relieve swelling; antihistamine dosed properly.

Animal bites
Clean any bleeding area; apply pressure until bleeding subsides; go to the vet.

Spider bites
Use cold compress and a pressurized pack to inhibit venom's spreading.

Antifreeze poisoning
Induce vomiting with hydrogen peroxide. Seek *immediate* veterinary help!

Fish hooks
Removal best handled by vet; hook must be cut in order to remove.

Snake bites
Pack ice around bite; contact vet quickly; identify snake for proper antivenin.

Car accident
Move dog from roadway with blanket; seek veterinary aid.

Shock
Calm the dog; keep him warm; seek immediate veterinary help.

Nosebleed
Apply cold compress to the nose; apply pressure to any visible abrasion.

Bleeding
Apply pressure above the area; treat wound by applying a cotton pack.

Heat stroke
Submerge dog in cold bath; cool down with fresh air and water; go to the vet.

Frostbite/Hypothermia
Warm the dog with a warm bath, electric blankets or hot water bottles.

Abrasions
Clean the wound and wash out thoroughly with fresh water; apply antiseptic.

!! *Remember: an injured dog may attempt to bite a helping hand from fear and confusion. Always muzzle the dog before trying to offer assistance.* **!!**

Recognizing a Sick Dog

Unlike colicky babies and cranky children, our canine kids cannot tell us when they are feeling ill. Therefore, there are a number of signs that owners can identify to know that their dogs are not feeling well.

Take note for physical manifestations such as:

- unusual, bad odor, including bad breath
- excessive shedding
- wax in the ears, chronic ear irritation
- oily, flaky, dull haircoat
- mucus, tearing or similar discharge in the eyes
- fleas or mites
- mucus in stool, diarrhea
- sensitivity to petting or handling
- licking at paws, scratching face, etc.

Keep an eye out for behavioral changes as well, including:

- lethargy, idleness
- lack of patience or general irritability
- lack of interest in food
- phobias (fear of people, loud noises, etc.)
- strange behavior, suspicion, fear
- coprophagia
- more frequent barking
- whimpering, crying

Get Well Soon

You don't need a DVM to provide good TLC to your sick or recovering dog, but you do need to pay attention to some details that normally wouldn't bother him. The following tips will aid Fido's recovery and get him back on his paws again:

- Keep his space free of irritating smells, like heavy perfumes and air fresheners.
- Rest is the best medicine! Avoid harsh lighting that will prevent your dog from sleeping. Shade him from bright sunlight during the day and dim the lights in the evening.
- Keep the noise level down. Animals are more sensitive to sound when they are sick.
- Be attentive to any necessary temperature adjustments. A dog with a fever needs a cool room and cold liquids. A bitch that is whelping or recovering from surgery will be more comfortable in a warm room, consuming warm liquids and food.
- You wouldn't send a sick child back to school early, so don't rush your dog back into a full routine until he seems absolutely ready.

Number-One Killer Disease in Dogs: CANCER

In every age, there is a word associated with a disease or plague that causes humans to shudder. In the 21st century, that word is "cancer." Just as cancer is the leading cause of death in humans, it claims nearly half the lives of dogs that die from a natural disease as well as half the dogs that die over the age of ten years.

Described as a genetic disease, cancer becomes a greater risk as the dog ages. Vets and dog owners have become increasingly aware of the threat of cancer to dogs. Statistics reveal that one dog in every five will develop cancer, the most common of which is skin cancer. Many cancers, including prostate, ovarian and breast cancer, can be avoided by spaying and neutering our dogs by the age of six months.

Early detection of cancer can save or extend a dog's life, so it is absolutely vital for owners to have their dogs examined by a qualified vet or oncologist immediately upon detection of any abnormality. Certain dietary guidelines have also proven to reduce the onset and spread of cancer. Foods based on fish rather than beef, due to the presence of Omega-3 fatty acids, are recommended. Other amino acids such as glutamine have significant benefits for canines, particularly those breeds that show a greater susceptibility to cancer.

Cancer management and treatments promise hope for future generations of canines. Since the disease is genetic, breeders should never breed a dog whose parents, grandparents and any related siblings have developed cancer. It is difficult to know whether to exclude an otherwise healthy dog from a breeding program, as the disease does not manifest itself until the dog's senior years.

RECOGNIZE CANCER WARNING SIGNS

Since early detection can possibly rescue your dog from becoming a cancer statistic, it is essential for owners to recognize the possible signs and seek the assistance of a qualified professional.

- Abnormal bumps or lumps that continue to grow
- Bleeding or discharge from any body cavity
- Persistent stiffness or lameness
- Recurrent sores or sores that do not heal
- Inappetence
- Breathing difficulties
- Weight loss
- Bad breath or odors
- General malaise and fatigue
- Eating and swallowing problems
- Difficulty urinating and defecating

Disease	Percentage
Cancer	47%
Heart disease	12%
Kidney disease	7%
Epilepsy	4%
Liver disease	4%
Bloat	3%
Diabetes	3%
Stroke	2%
Cushing's disease	2%
Immune diseases	2%
Other causes	14%

The Ten Most Common Fatal Diseases in Pure-bred Dogs

CDS: COGNITIVE DYSFUNCTION SYNDROME
"Old-Dog Syndrome"

There are many ways for you to evaluate old-dog syndrome. Veterinarians have defined CDS (cognitive dysfunction syndrome) as the gradual deterioration of cognitive abilities. These are indicated by changes in the dog's behavior. When a dog changes his routine response, and maladies have been eliminated as the cause of these behavioral changes, then CDS is the usual diagnosis.

More than half the dogs over eight years old suffer from some form of CDS. The older the dog, the more chance he has of suffering from CDS. In humans, doctors often dismiss the CDS behavioral changes as part of "winding down."

There are four major signs of CDS: frequent potty accidents inside the home, sleeping much more or much less than normal, acting confused and failing to respond to social stimuli.

SYMPTOMS OF CDS

FREQUENT POTTY ACCIDENTS
- *Urinates in the house.*
- *Defecates in the house.*
- *Doesn't signal that he wants to go out.*

SLEEP PATTERNS
- *Awakens more slowly.*
- *Sleeps more than normal during the day.*
- *Sleeps less during the night.*

CONFUSION
- *Goes outside and just stands there.*
- *Appears confused with a faraway look in his eyes.*
- *Hides more often.*
- *Doesn't recognize friends.*
- *Doesn't come when called.*
- *Walks around listlessly and without a destination.*

FAILURE TO RESPOND TO SOCIAL STIMULI
- *Comes to people less frequently, whether called or not.*
- *Doesn't tolerate petting for more than a short time.*
- *Doesn't come to the door when you return home.*

ITALIAN GREYHOUND

The term *old* is a qualitative term. For dogs, as well as for their masters, old is relative. Certainly we can all distinguish between a puppy Italian Greyhound and an adult Italian Greyhound—there are the obvious physical traits, such as size, appearance and facial expressions, and personality traits. Puppies and young dogs like to play with children. Children's natural exuberance is a good match for the seemingly endless energy of young dogs. They like to run, jump, chase and retrieve. When dogs grow older and cease their interaction with children, they are often thought of as being too old to keep pace with the kids. On the other hand, if an Italian Greyhound is only exposed to people with quieter lifestyles, his life will normally be less active and the decrease in his activity level as he ages will not be as obvious.

If people live to be 100 years old, dogs live to be 20 years old. While this might seem like a good rule of thumb, it is very inaccurate. When trying to compare dog years to human years, you cannot make a generalization about all dogs. You can make the generalization that 14 years is a good lifespan for an Italian Greyhound, though some lucky (and well-cared-for) Italian Greyhounds have lived to 20 years. Few breeds can boast such longevity, and the Toy breeds, in general, are blest with the longest lifespans.

A more accurate, but still very general, rule of thumb is that the first three years of a dog's life are like seven times that of a comparable human. That means a 3-year-old dog is like a 21-year-old human. As the curve of comparison shows, however, there is no hard and fast rule for comparing dog and human ages. As you know, small breeds tend to live longer than large breeds; additionaly, some breeds' adolescent periods last longer than others' and some breeds experience rapid periods of growth. The comparison is made even more difficult, for, likewise, not all humans age at the same rate...and human females tend to live longer than human males.

WHAT TO LOOK FOR IN SENIORS

Most veterinarians and behaviorists use the seven-year mark as the time to consider a dog a senior. The term "senior" does not imply that the dog is geriatric and has begun to fail in mind and body. Aging is essentially a slowing process. Humans readily admit that they feel a difference in their activity level from age 20 to 30, and then from 30 to 40, etc. By treating the seven-year-old dog as a senior, owners are able to implement certain therapeutic and preventative medical strategies with the help of their veterinarians. A senior-care program should include at least two veterinary visits per year and screening sessions to determine the dog's health status, as well as nutritional counseling. Veterinarians determine the senior dog's health status through a blood smear for a complete blood count, serum chemistry profile with electrolytes, urinalysis, blood pressure check, electrocardiogram, ocular tonometry (pressure on the eyeball) and dental prophylaxis.

Such an extensive program for senior dogs is well advised before owners start to see the obvious physical signs of aging, such as slower and inhibited movement, graying, increased sleep/nap periods and disinterest in play and other activity. This preventative program promises a longer, healthier life for the aging

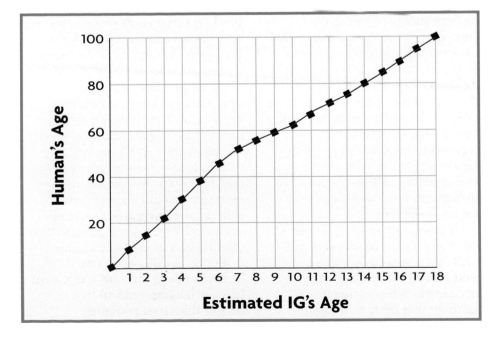

dog. Among the physical problems common in aging dogs are the loss of sight and hearing, arthritis, kidney and liver failure, diabetes mellitus, heart disease and Cushing's disease (a hormonal disease).

In addition to the physical manifestations discussed, there are some behavioral changes and problems related to aging dogs. Dogs suffering from hearing or vision loss, dental discomfort or arthritis can become aggressive. Likewise, the near-deaf and/or blind dog may be startled more easily and react in an unexpectedly aggressive manner. Seniors suffering from senility can become more impatient and irritable. Housesoiling accidents are associated with loss of mobility, kidney problems and loss of sphincter control as well as plaque accumulation, physiological brain changes and reactions to medications. Older dogs, just like young puppies, can suffer from separation anxiety, which can lead to excessive barking, whining, housesoiling and destructive behavior. Seniors may become fearful of everyday sounds, such as vacuum cleaners, heaters, thunder and passing traffic. Some dogs have difficulty sleeping, due to discomfort, the need for frequent potty visits and the like.

Owners should avoid spoiling the older dog with too many

NOTICING THE SYMPTOMS
The symptoms listed below are symptoms that gradually appear and become more noticeable. They are not life-threatening; however, the symptoms below are to be taken very seriously and warrant a discussion with your veterinarian:
- Your dog cries and whimpers when he moves, and he stops running completely.
- Convulsions start or become more serious and frequent. The usual convulsion (spasm) is when the dog stiffens and starts to tremble, being unable or unwilling to move. The seizure usually lasts for 5 to 30 minutes.
- Your dog drinks more water and urinates more frequently. Wetting and bowel accidents take place indoors without warning.
- Vomiting becomes more and more frequent.

treats. Obesity is a common problem in older dogs and subtracts years from their lives. Keep the senior dog as trim as possible, since excess weight puts additional stress on the body's vital organs. Some breeders recommend supplementing the diet with foods high in fiber and lower in calories. Adding fresh vegetables and marrow broth to the senior's diet makes a tasty, low-calorie, low-fat supplement.

Vets also offer specialty diets for senior dogs that are worth exploring.

Your dog, as he nears his twilight years, needs your patience and good care more than ever. Never punish an older dog for an accident or abnormal behavior. For all the years of love, protection and companionship that your dog has provided, he deserves special attention and courtesies. The older dog may need to relieve himself at 3 a.m. because he can no longer "hold it" for eight hours. Older dogs may not be able to remain crated for more than two or three hours. Although he may not seem as enthusiastic about your attention and petting, he does appreciate the considerations you offer as he gets older.

Your Italian Greyhound does not understand why his world is slowing down. Owners must make their dogs' transition into their golden years as pleasant and rewarding as possible.

WHAT TO DO WHEN THE TIME COMES

You are never fully prepared to make a rational decision about putting your dog to sleep. It is very obvious that you love your Italian Greyhound or you would not be reading this book. Putting a beloved dog to sleep is extremely difficult. It is a decision that must be made with your veterinarian. You are usually forced to make the decision when your dog experiences one or more life-threatening symptoms, requiring you to seek veterinary help.

If the prognosis of the malady indicates that the end is near and that your beloved pet will only continue to suffer and experience no enjoyment for the balance of his life, then euthanasia is the right choice.

WHAT IS EUTHANASIA?

Euthanasia derives from the Greek, meaning *good death*. In other words, it means the planned, painless killing of a dog suffering from a painful, incurable condition, or who is so aged that he cannot walk, see, eat or control his excretory functions.

CONSISTENCY COUNTS

Puppies and older dogs are very similar in their need for consistency in their lives. Older pets may experience hearing and vision loss, or may just be more easily confused by changes in their homes. Try to keep things consistent for the senior dog. For example, doors that are always open or closed should remain so. Most importantly, don't dismiss a pet just because he's getting old; most senior dogs remain active and important parts of their owners' lives.

Euthanasia is usually accomplished by injection with an overdose of anesthesia or a barbiturate. Aside from the prick of the needle, the experience is usually painless.

MAKING THE DECISION

The decision to euthanize your dog is never easy. The days during which the dog becomes ill and the end occurs can be unusually stressful for you. If this is your first experience with the death of a loved one, you may need the comfort dictated by your religious beliefs. If you are the head of the family and have children, you should have involved them in the decision of putting your Italian Greyhound to sleep. Usually your dog can be maintained on drugs for a few days at the veterinarian's clinic in order to give you ample time to make a decision. During this time, talking with members of your family, with clergy or with

There likely will be a pet cemetery in your locality. This is one of your options if you choose to memorialize you beloved IG.

people who have lived through the same experience can ease the burden of your inevitable decision.

THE FINAL RESTING PLACE

Dogs can have some of the same privileges as humans. The remains of your beloved dog can be buried in a pet cemetery, which is generally expensive. A dog who has died at home can be buried in your yard in a place suitably marked with a special stone or a newly planted tree or bush. Alternatively, your dog can be cremated individually and the ashes returned to you. A less expensive option is mass cremation, although, of course, the ashes of individual dogs cannot then be returned. Vets can usually help you with the final arrangements. The cost of these options should always be discussed frankly and openly with your veterinarian.

GETTING ANOTHER DOG?

The grief of losing your beloved dog will be as lasting as the grief of losing a human friend or relative. In most cases, if your dog died of old age (if there is such a thing), he had slowed down considerably. Do you now want a new Italian Greyhound puppy? Or are you better off finding a more mature Italian Greyhound, say two to three years of age, which will usually be house-

In most pet cemeteries, there are special areas in which urns containing dogs' ashes can be stored.

trained and will have an already developed personality. In this case, you can find out if you like each other after a few hours of being together.

The decision is, of course, your own. Do you want another Italian Greyhound or perhaps a different breed so as to avoid comparison with your beloved friend? Most people usually choose the same breed because they know and love the characteristics of that breed. Then, too, they often know people who have the same breed and perhaps they are lucky enough that a breeder they know and respect expects a litter soon. What could be better?

TALK IT OUT
The more openly your family discusses the whole stressful occurrence of the aging and eventual loss of a beloved pet, the easier it will be for you when the time comes.

ITALIAN GREYHOUND

If you purchased an Italian Greyhound puppy with definite plans to show him, then you will have informed the breeder of your intentions and taken his advice about the pup's show potential. Not every Italian Greyhound puppy will grow up to be a show-dog candidate, so the breeder's input and advice are critical to your potential success in conformation showing.

To the novice, exhibiting an IG in the show ring may look easy, but it takes a lot of hard work and devotion to do top winning at a show such as the prestigious Westminster Kennel Club, not to mention a little luck too!

The first concept that the canine novice learns when watching a dog show is that each dog first competes against members of his own breed. Once the judge has selected the best member of each breed (Best of Breed), provided that the show is judged on a Group system, that chosen dog will compete with other dogs in his group. Finally, the dogs chosen first in each group will compete for Best in Show.

The second concept that you must understand is that the dogs are not actually compared against one another. The judge compares each dog against the standard for the breed. While some early breed standards were indeed based on specific dogs that were famous or popular, many dedicated enthusiasts say that a perfect specimen, as described in the standard, has never walked into a

CLUB CONTACTS

You can get information about dog shows from the national kennel clubs:

American Kennel Club
5580 Centerview Dr., Raleigh, NC 27606-3390
www.akc.org

United Kennel Club
100 E. Kilgore Road, Kalamazoo, MI 49002
www.ukcdogs.com

Canadian Kennel Club
89 Skyway Ave., Suite 100, Etobicoke
Ontario
M9W 6R4, Canada
www.ckc.ca

The Kennel Club
1-5 Clarges St., Piccadilly
London W1Y 8AB, UK
www.the-kennel-club.org.uk

show ring, has never been bred and, to the woe of dog breeders around the globe, does not exist. Breeders attempt to get as close to this ideal as possible with every litter, but theoretically the "perfect" dog is so elusive that it is impossible.

If you are interested in exploring the world of dog showing, your best bet is to join your local breed club or the national parent club, which is the Italian Greyhound Club of America (IGCA). The IGCA and local clubs host specialty shows in which only Italian Greyhounds can compete. The National Specialty is held by the IGCA annually, and its location changes each year. Specialties are exciting for fanciers and fans alike, as they can include not only conformation classes but also obedience trials, lure coursing and more! Clubs also send out newsletters, and some organize training days and seminars in order that people may learn more about their chosen breed. To locate the breed club closest to you, contact the American Kennel Club, which furnishes the rules and regulations for all of these events plus general dog registration and other basic requirements of dog ownership.

If your Italian Greyhound is of age and registered, you can enter him in a dog show where the breed is offered classes. Only

SHOW-QUALITY SHOWS

While you may purchase a puppy in the hope of having a successful career in the show ring, it is impossible to tell, at ten to twelve weeks of age, whether your dog will be a contender. Some promising pups end up with minor to serious faults that prevent them from taking home an award, but this certainly does not mean they can't be the best of companions for you and your family. To find out if your potential show dog is show-quality, enter him in a match to see how a judge evaluates him. You may also take him back to your breeder as he matures to see what he might advise.

BECOMING A CHAMPION

An official AKC champion of record requires that a dog accumulate 15 points under three different judges, including two "majors" under different judges. Points are awarded based on the number of dogs entered into competition, varying from breed to breed and place to place. A win of three, four or five points is considered a "major." The AKC annually assigns a schedule of points to adjust to the variations that accompany a breed's popularity and the population of a given area.

Small breeds like the IG are examined by the judge on a table. You can practice at home on your gooming table so that your IG is not startled by the process.

unaltered dogs can be entered in a dog show, so if you have spayed or neutered your Italian Greyhound, you cannot compete in conformation shows. The reason for this is simple. Dog shows are the main forum to

prove which representatives in a breed are worthy of being bred. Only dogs that have proven themselves in the show ring by attaining a Champion title—the recognized "seal of approval" for excellence in pure-bred dogs—should be bred. Altered dogs, however, can participate in other events such as obedience trials and the Canine Good Citizen® program, although not in lure coursing.

Before you actually step into the ring, you would be well advised to sit back and observe the judge's ring procedure. If it is your first time in the ring, do not be over-anxious and run to the front of the line. It is much better to stand back and study how the exhibitor in front of you is performing. The judge asks each handler to "stack" the dog, hopefully showing the dog off to his best advantage. The judge will observe the dog from a distance and from different angles, and approach the dog to check his teeth, overall structure, alertness and muscle tone, as well as consider how well the dog "conforms" to the standard. Most importantly, the judge will have the exhibitor move the dog around the ring in some pattern that he should specify. Finally, the judge will give the dog one last look before moving on to the next exhibitor.

If you are not in the top four in your class at your first show, do not be discouraged. Be patient

after the Associated Sheep, Police, Army Dog Society of Great Britain. Since the days of Mrs. Walker, obedience trials have grown by leaps and bounds, and today there are over 2,000 trials held in the US every year, with more than 100,000 dogs competing. Any AKC-registered dog can enter an obedience trial, regardless of conformational disqualifications or neutering.

Obedience trials are divided into three levels of progressive difficulty. At the first level, the Novice, dogs compete for the title Companion Dog (CD); at the intermediate level, the Open, dogs compete for the title Companion

The high-stepping regal prance of the IG is an important breed characteristic. Dogs of all breeds are moved around the ring at shows so that their gait can be appraised.

and consistent, and you may eventually find yourself in a winning line-up. Remember that the winners were once in your shoes and have devoted many hours and much money to earn the placement. If you find that your dog is losing every time and never getting a nod, it may be time to consider a different dog sport or to just enjoy your Italian Greyhound as a pet.

OBEDIENCE TRIALS

Obedience trials in the US trace back to the early 1930s when organized obedience training was developed to demonstrate how well dog and owner could work together. The pioneer of obedience trials is Mrs. Helen Whitehouse Walker, a Standard Poodle fancier, who designed a series of exercises

JUNIOR SHOWMANSHIP

For budding dog handlers, ages 10 to 18 years, Junior Showmanship competitions are an excellent training ground for the next generation of dog professionals. Owning and caring for a dog are wonderful methods of teaching children responsibility, and Junior Showmanship builds upon that foundation. Juniors learn by grooming, handling and training their dogs, and the quality of junior's presentation of the dog (and himself) is evaluated by a licensed judge. The junior can enter with any registered AKC dog to compete, including an ILP, provided that the dog lives with him or a member of his family.

AMERICAN KENNEL CLUB TITLES

The AKC offers over 40 different titles to dogs in competition. Depending on the events that your dog can enter, different titles apply. Some titles can be applied as prefixes, meaning that they are placed before the dog's name (e.g., Ch. King of the Road) and others are used as suffixes, placed after the dog's name (e.g., King of the Road, CD).

These titles are used as prefixes:

Conformation Dog Shows
- Ch. (Champion)

Obedience Trials
- NOC (National Obedience Champion)
- OTCH (Obedience Trial Champion)
- VCCH (Versatile Companion Champion)

Tracking Tests
- CT [Champion Tracker (TD,TDX and VST)]

Agility Trials
- MACH (Master Agility Champion)
- MACH2, MACH3, MACH4, etc.

Field Trials
- FC (Field Champion)
- AFC (Amateur Field Champion)
- NFC (National Field Champion)
- NAFC (National Amateur Field Champion)
- NOGDC (National Open Gun Dog Champion)
- AKC GDSC (AKC Gun Dog Stake Champion)
- AKC RGDSC (AKC Retrieving Gun Dog Stake Champion)

Herding Trials
- HC (Herding Champion)

Dual
- DC (Dual Champion — Ch. and FC)

Triple
- TC (Triple Champion — Ch., FC and OTCH)

Coonhounds
- NCH (Nite Champion)
- GNCH (Grand Nite Champion)
- SHNCH (Senior Grand Nite Champion)
- GCH (Senior Champion)
- SGCH (Senior Grand Champion)
- GFC (Grand Field Champion)
- SGFC (Senior Grand Field Champion)
- WCH (Water Race Champion)
- GWCH (Water Race Grand Champion)
- SGWCH (Senior Grand Water Race Champion)

These titles are used as suffixes:

Obedience
- CD (Companion Dog)
- CDX (Companion Dog Excellent)
- UD (Utility Dog)
- UDX (Utility Dog Excellent)
- VCD1 (Versatile Companion Dog 1)
- VCD2 (Versatile Companion Dog 2)
- VCD3 (Versatile Companion Dog 3)
- VCD4 (Versatile Companion Dog 4)

Tracking Tests
- TD (Tracking Dog)
- TDX (Tracking Dog Excellent)
- VST (Variable Surface Tracker)

Agility Trials
- NA (Novice Agility)
- OA (Open Agility)
- AX (Agility Excellent)
- MX (Master Agility Excellent)
- NAJ (Novice Jumpers with weaves)
- OAJ (Open Jumpers with weaves)
- AXJ (Excellent Jumpers with weaves)
- MXJ (Master Excellent Jumpers with weaves)

Hunting Test
- JH (Junior Hunter)
- SH (Senior Hunter)
- MH (Master Hunter)

Herding Test
- HT (Herding Tested)
- PT (Pre-Trial Tested)
- HS (Herding Started)
- HI (Herding Intermediate)
- HX (Herding Excellent)

Lure Coursing
- JC (Junior Courser)
- SC (Senior Courser)
- MC (Master Courser)

Earthdog
- JE (Junior Earthdog)
- SE (Senior Earthdog)
- ME (Master Earthdog)

Dog Excellent (CDX); and at the advanced level, the Utility, dogs compete for the title Utility Dog (UD). Classes are sub-divided into "A" (for beginners) and "B" (for more experienced handlers). A perfect score at any level is 200, and a dog must score 170 or better to earn a "leg," of which three are needed to earn the title. To earn points, the dog must score more than 50% of the available points in each exercise; the possible points range from 20 to 40.

Each level consists of a different set of exercises. In the Novice level, the dog must heel on- and off-lead, come, long sit, long down and stand for examination. These skills are the basic ones required for a well-behaved "Companion Dog." The Open level requires that the dog perform the same exercises as in the Novice but without a leash for extended lengths of time, as well as retrieve a dumbbell, broad jump and drop on recall. In the Utility level, dogs must perform ten difficult exercises, including scent discrimination, hand signals for basic commands, directed jump and directed retrieve.

Once a dog has earned the UD title, he can compete with other proven obedience dogs for the coveted title of Utility Dog Excellent (UDX), which requires that the dog win "legs" in ten shows. Utility Dogs who earn "legs" in Open B and Utility B earn points toward their Obedience Trial Champion title. In 1977, the title Obedience Trial Champion (OTCh.) was established by the AKC. To become an OTCh., a dog needs to earn 100 points, which requires three first places in Open B and Utility under three different judges.

NEATNESS COUNTS

Surely you've spent hours grooming your dog to perfection for the show ring, but don't forget about yourself! While the dog should be the center of attention, it is important that you also appear neat and clean. Wear smart, appropriate clothes and comfortable shoes in a color that contrasts with your dog's coat. Look and act like a professional.

AGILITY TRIALS

Having had its origins in the UK back in 1977, AKC agility had its official beginning in the US in August 1994, when the first licensed agility trials were held. The AKC allows all registered breeds to participate, providing the dog is 12 months of age or older. Agility is designed so that the handler demonstrates how well the dog can work at his side. The handler directs his dog over an obstacle course that includes jumps (similar to those used in obedience trials), as well as tires, the dog walk, weave poles, pipe tunnels, collapsed tunnels, etc. While working his way through the course, the dog must keep one eye and ear on the handler and the rest of his body on the course. The handler gives verbal and hand signals to guide the dog through the course.

The first organization to promote agility trials in the US was the United States Dog Agility Association, Inc. (USDAA), which was established in 1986 and spawned numerous member clubs around the country; dogs must be at least 18 months old to compete in USDAA events. Both the USDAA and the AKC offer titles to winning dogs. Three titles are available through the USDAA: Agility Dog (AD), Advanced

Italian Greyhounds usually do very well in agility because of their natural talents for running, jumping and climbing.

Agility Dog (AAD) and Master Agility Dog (MAD). The AKC offers Novice Agility (NA), Open Agility (OA), Agility Excellent (AX) and Master Agility Excellent (MX). Beyond these four AKC titles, dogs can win additional ones in "jumper" classes, Jumpers with Weave Novice (NAJ), Open (OAJ) and Excellent (MXJ), which lead to the ultimate title(s): MACH, Master Agility Champion. Dogs can continue to add number designations to the MACH titles, indicating how many times the dog has met the MACH requirements, such as MACH1, MACH2 and so forth.

Agility is great fun for dog and owner, with many rewards for everyone involved. Interested owners should join a training club that has obstacles and experienced agility handlers who can introduce you and your dog to the "ropes" (and tires, tunnels, etc.).

LURE COURSING
Sighthound owners are fortunate to have the chance to try their dogs at lure coursing! Coursing events have been popular around the world, with many famous races beginning in England, such as the Waterloo Cup for Greyhounds that dates back to 1836. The sport of lure coursing in the US is a much more recent phenomenon, having begun in the 1970s by gazehound fancier Lyle Gillette and some hunting enthusiasts. Since hunting in open fields is fairly dangerous, and not common or legal in many places, the need for a simulated event arose and lure coursing was the answer. Lure coursing allows owners to give their dogs a forum to test their field abilities without actually working an open field in pursuit of jackrabbits or the like. Usually these events use plastic bags or white fur dummies, which give the dog the impression of game escaping through the course. Dogs are scored based on how well they follow the lure, their enthusiasm for the chase and their agility, speed and endurance.

The American Kennel Club sanctions lure coursing for the Italian Greyhound's larger cousins, namely the other sighthound breeds, but not for the IG. There are other events that are sponsored by breed clubs, though AKC titles cannot be earned. For safety's sake, dogs are required to be one year of age or older in order to participate, and unlike obedience trials, dogs must not have any disqualifying fault, which includes spaying and neutering.

AKC offers three suffix titles to winning dogs, including Junior Courser (JC), Senior Courser (SC) and Master Courser (MC); the most prestigious AKC title is the prefix Field Champion (FC). There are also non-competitive events sponsored by affiliated clubs, fun-

The world's oldest dog show is the Westminster Kennel Club Dog Show, which takes place annually in New York City. The Group finals are completely televised, and the show has an attendance of more than 50,000 people per day.

Climbing the A-frame is a talented IG, who accomplishes the task with considerable grace. Competing in agility trials is one of the great pleasures of owning an Italian Greyhound.

filled meets that are ideal for the novice courser.

The AKC National Lure Coursing Championship is the annual event where the best of the best sighthounds from around the country come together to compete. This two-day event usually attracts over 100 titled sight hounds, including many Dual Champions and Field Champions. The qualifications to participate are steep and include a Best of Breed or three-point "major" win at a Regional or Championship event. The event moves to different venues each year but always proves to be the most exciting coursing event of the year.

Field trials also are held every weekend by organizations like the American Sighthound Field Association (ASFA), which has over 100 member clubs. Newcomers are encouraged to visit the club's website (www.asfa.org) to locate local clubs and to contact one of the regional directors, who can assist

CANINE GOOD CITIZEN® PROGRAM

Have you ever considered getting your dog "certified"? The AKC's Canine Good Citizen® Program affords your dog just that opportunity. Your dog shows that he is a well-behaved canine citizen, using the basic training and good manners you have taught him, by taking a series of ten tests that illustrate that he can behave properly at home, in a public place and around other dogs. The tests are administered by participating dog clubs, colleges, 4-H clubs, scouts and other community groups and are open to all pure-bred and mixed-breed dogs. Upon passing the ten tests, the suffix CGC is then applied to your dog's name.

The ten tests are: 1. Accepting a friendly stranger; 2. Sitting politely for petting; 3. Appearance and grooming; 4. Walking on a lead; 5. Walking through a group of people; 6. Sit, down and stay on command; 7. Coming when called; 8. Meeting another dog; 9. Calm reaction to distractions; 10. Separation from owner.

interested parties in getting started in lure coursing.

Sighthounds at ASFA coursing events will run the designated course twice, with the scores from each run combined to determine a final score. Based on how many dogs compete and where the dog completes the course, the dog is awarded placements and points. The ASFA awards a Field Champion title to any dog that earns 100 points and two first places (or two seconds and one first places). Beyond this title, a dog can earn a Lure Courser of Merit title for further accomplishments.

When viewing the IG moving at full tilt, there is no doubt that running is still in this dog's blood.

INDEX

Page numbers in **boldface** indicate illustrations.

My Italian Greyhound

PUT YOUR PUPPY'S FIRST PICTURE HERE

Dog's Name _____

Date _____ Photographer _____